Boo & Patch: A Tail of Hope

-

The First Adventure
by
Gary Boardman

Copyright

BOO & PATCH: A TAIL OF HOPE was first published in Great Britain in 2026.

Available in Paperback and eBook.

ISBN: 978-1-9195301-0-9
Stellar Life

Acknowledgements

This book is dedicated to my loving family, whose unwavering support and encouragement made it possible.

When my son was younger, I used to make up bedtime stories.
He loved them all, eagerly awaiting new adventures every night.

To keep up with his growing imagination, I created a character called Boo and his trusty sidekick, Patch. Together, they embarked on wild adventures and solved strange mysteries. The moment Boo and Patch were born; they became his nightly request. From then on, every night was a Boo and Patch night.

It was my family who encouraged me to bring these characters to life, inspiring and supporting me to become a writer. This story exists because they believed in me. My hope is that other children will enjoy Boo and Patch's adventures just as much as my son did.

Behind every great story is a dedicated editor, and I'm deeply grateful to Deborah Jean White for her invaluable guidance, encouragement, and, most importantly, her belief in Boo and Patch. Her expertise and support have made this journey truly unforgettable.

Thank you to everyone who has picked up this book. I hope you enjoy the adventure as much as I have enjoyed writing it.

For my son.
You are my greatest adventure.
Wherever your journey leads,
Walk it with courage, friendship and a good heart.

Chapter One

Springtime Saturdays were the best. The weekend meant freedom. A chance to dive into whatever adventures I could dream up. The possibilities were endless and today was without a doubt the start of something epic.

I sat up in bed. The walls surrounding me were covered with posters of explorers and adventurers. They greeted me, like every other morning, but today felt different. I felt an itch for something more... something exciting.

'Jake, are you up? Do you want breakfast?' my foster Mum Joyce called from downstairs. The lovely smell of something half sweet and half burnt wafted through my bedroom door. That meant only one thing: Joyce's badly cooked waffles and pancakes were on the kitchen table. A little crispy here and there, but still the best breakfast a hungry boy like me could wish for.

Not wasting time, I sprang out of bed like a kangaroo on caffeine, throwing my beloved 'spy guy' themed bedding onto the floor and army-rolling over the bed towards my 'spy guy' slippers.

Like most other pre-teen boys, I had an unstoppable craving for adventure, a monster of an imagination, bundles of energy and a sucker for a brand. (I turned off my 'spy guy' lamp and stopped my 'spy guy' alarm, which was now screaming, 'Attack the Day Adventurer...' on repeat).

I followed the smell of home cooking from the kitchen. I took the usual course, which included hurdling soft toys outside my door, zig-zagging through the building-block minefield and tiptoeing by George's room. I could hear him snoring without a care in the world. To be honest, when he arrived, I was one hundred percent sure that I would be sent away once they had 'one of their own'. Yet it didn't happen. It would seem that I was lovable enough to keep around.

I glanced at our full-length mirror.

'You're looking good,' I said to myself, running my hand through my thick, mousey-coloured hair as if my fingers were a comb. I knew I looked like my real Mum. My Grammy Constance told me enough times, so I knew it was true.

'No matter what happens, remember your family loves you,' Grammy's words echoed in my head. My real mum's final words apparently. I held onto these words for years, wondering if they meant anything. Sometimes the words made my head hurt. Made me want to cry into my pillow. Made me feel trapped.

Maybe that's why I always felt so restless, why I craved adventure and exploration. I couldn't shake the feeling that there was something more out there, a clue or a sign that would lead me to the truth about my parents. The life I could have had. It was as if the big wide world was a puzzle, and I was put on this planet to find the missing pieces.

I ran my hand through my hair again, noticing a tear escaping down my cheek. I swiped it away. The ache of missing them was always there, just rumbling under the surface, like a crying volcano, but I was not a crybaby.

Around the corner of the landing and heading for the stairs, I stopped dead in my tracks. I saw it! A rare, golden opportunity. No clothes blocked my way, and no one was watching. It was just too good an opportunity to miss.

Boom! I went for it. I jumped on the banister and gave myself an almighty push. I was soon sliding down with my hands in the air, pretending I was on some crazy rollercoaster. This was the rush of excitement I needed to take away all that emotional stuff.

'Wheeeeee!'

I really hadn't thought through this plan. As I curled around the staircase and into the final descent, I noticed a problem looming on the horizon. No, No, No! It can't be. George's little pram was sitting at the bottom (like it knew I would be coming).

It was too late.

Before I had time to react, I had already shot off the end like an express train.

Peter, my foster Dad, opened the front door on cue. Typical! He was returning from his morning run, sporting steamed-up glasses and sweating in an unnecessarily tight, two sizes too small neon jogging suit.

'Move!' I screamed.

He jumped to the side and watched in surprise as I, 'his foster kid' surfed his son's pram straight past him through the opening. I zoomed down the path and crashed straight into Joyce's beautiful rose bush in the centre of the garden.

I looked back only to see my foster dad shrugging his shoulders and rolling his eyes.

'Jake, when are you going to learn?'

Then the pain hit. It hit all over my body like a million-billion bee stings. Peter rescued me from the rose bush and marched me into the kitchen towards Joyce.

There was a sigh of acceptance as she plucked the prickly thorns from my body. They knew this wasn't the first time I had got in a pickle since I had arrived and certainly guaranteed not to be the last.

'Oh, Boo! Why? Oh, why?' Joyce asked as she pulled some extra-long thorns from my fleshy bits. In the end, I was so full of red holes that I looked like I was on a second wave of chicken pox. 'Why oh, why Boo?' she repeated.

Oh wait. Let me explain to you... the reader - Jake is my real name, but everyone refers to me as Boo. You see when my real great Grammy (who was invited to most family events, agreed by social services) was dozing off in her comfy armchair I saw it as a golden opportunity. I was wearing a realistic glow-in-the-dark ghost costume and couldn't wait to find some prey to scare. Unfortunately for Grammy, she was on the hit list. I could see her stirring, so I jumped out from behind the sofa with an almighty, 'Boooo!'

She jumped so high out of the chair she almost hit the ceiling. Her false teeth flew out of her mouth.

'Aghhh!' I screamed.

Grammy simply gave her teeth a quick dunk in her lemonade and popped them straight back into her mouth without a second thought.

'Oh, my little Boo,' she muttered as she settled back in her armchair, and everyone laughed.

From then on, it stuck.

'Ouch!' I screamed as Joyce pulled out the last thorn bringing me back to reality. The pain was unbearable, yet I sat still and let her rip with the antiseptic spray. I smelled like a hospital.

I'm sure Peter, who I will now refer to as Dad, half enjoyed watching me wince as Joyce, who I will now refer to as Mum, dabbed me with soaked cotton balls of pain. In truth, I had a history of unfortunate events mixed with strange happenings, so their life was never going to be dull from the moment they fostered me. I seemed to attract the unexpected, from falling down a well to constantly wandering off and getting lost.

'Did you want breakfast, Boo?' Mum asked kindly.

'Yes, please,' I whispered, as I slowly sprawled out on the sofa, wincing with the prickly pain.

Chapter Two

The ground rumbled under my feet. The whole floor beneath my feet caved in, dropping me into the deep cavern below.

'Am I alive?' I cried out and my words echoed into the darkness.

The sounds of scurrying rats scared me.

I gasped for air.

Bruised and battered, I wiped the mud and creepy crawlies off my body.

'Where the heck am I?' I said into the darkness.

It was wet and cold, and a dank, mouldy smell wafted all around. Water dripped from above, sploshing into the surface of a pool of muddy water.

'Where am I?' I whispered again, as I squeezed my eyes shut.

And how am I going to get out?

I rummaged around in my coat pocket grabbing my old trusty pocket flashlight. Fortunately, I could now see, but unfortunately, I was undoubtedly trapped. A large, cold, dark, four-walled mud chamber was my prison.

Without wasting any time, I reached up to the wall opening and peered inside. A small dirt tunnel lay ahead. I jumped inside. My nerves were dancing with distress as the walls grew tighter around me. There was no turning back now.

'Yuck!' I yelled just before the tunnel abruptly widened, releasing its grip on me and sliding me sharply down a slope. I tumbled into another empty room.

Dead End! Nowhere obvious to go! Eternal darkness and despair ran wild within my mind as it gripped my nerves tightly.

I knew I needed to chill.

I took a deep breath.

How did I end up here?

Tears welled up in my eyes, but I wiped them away with the back of my hand. 'I have to get out of here,' I whispered into the darkness. 'I can't let this be the end.'

A faint glow came from my wrist. The ordinary hoop of glass my grandmother had given me, started to spark like mini solar flares blasting from the sun.

'What in the world?' I asked.

Looking down in shock, an inscription read, 'Let the light guide you in the darkness'.

Was it guiding me to safety?

I burrowed into the cold, moist earth. It was soft to the touch and easily displaced. I created a boy sized rabbit hole, tunnelling deeper into the unknown.

With a final shove, my numb hands finally broke through. A vacuum of empty space greeted me from the other side, and I could feel a peculiar change in temperature from freezing to a gentle calm warmth.

'This is awesome!' I said. But it wasn't awesome as it wasn't the exit I had wished for. Just another antechamber. I couldn't hide my disappointment as I landed on my knees.

'Where on earth am I now?' I spluttered out. It was a while before I allowed myself to look up. My eyes were now adjusting to a new room, which was as dank and lifeless as before. This time, there was an unusual, piled up mound of dirt up to waist height. Next to this, a shadowy figure....

Relief washed over me as I realised it was only the remains of a skeleton.

'Probably been stuck down here for years,' I whispered, 'Poor soul.'

My bracelet had obviously led me here for a reason, but a crusty old corpse and pile of mud weren't much of a path to freedom.

'What on earth?' I exclaimed, 'Arghh, it's moving.' I fell back in absolute shock.

The mound had sprung to life, and whatever had been lying dormant proceeded to hurtle around the room in a crazy spin—spraying dust and dirt in every direction. Could it be some sort of strange cave-dwelling creature?

Eventually, the beast seemed to run out of energy and came to a standstill, panting wildly. While the dust settled, it became clear what savage monster had caused the commotion.

'A dog,' I blurted out, questioning my own sanity at this point.

It was now sitting, staring blankly at the skeleton as if it was waiting for instructions from its old master. Sadly, no instructions came.

I rubbed my eyes in disbelief. How could this be?

The dog was now lying there, whimpering at the lifeless bones before him. He let out a bellowing howl of sadness before he turned to me.

'Where'd you come from, little fella?' I asked as I reached out to give the dog a warm, reassuring embrace. 'What's your story? This was your owner, huh? Poor doggie. How did you both end up here? This place is a nightmare.'

I hugged the dog tightly. 'It looks like we're both in a trap.'

The dog decided to launch forward and tunnelled into the dirt. He pulled out an old, leather, cylindrical-shaped container and placed it at my feet.

'What have you got there?' I asked.

It was an old, mysterious scroll case with a distinct goldenseal containing an emblem. Two planets on either side, connected by some glowing wavy symbols between them.

Intricate etched carvings of what seemed to be a traveller and his four-legged animal companion, portraying the stories of adventures they shared, embodied the casing. Examining closer, I looked back at the dog. It didn't take a genius to work out that they must be the same.

'How are you still alive?' I whispered, totally bewildered. A dog frozen in time, waiting for someone to set him free. It just didn't make sense. I shuddered and then looked again at the case. Gazing upon its beauty, I noticed the drawings began to animate like a cartoon springing to life, revolving across the leather depicting short memoirs of a past life. Little broken fragments hidden in the mist:

Of beginnings: a little puppy given to a young boy and the happiness they shared.

Of friendship: the lasting bond between them as they grew up together.

Of great travels: faraway lands beyond his wildest imagination and taking on thrilling adventures.

Of heroism: defeating mythical creatures and overcoming evil.

Of sadness: when their bond was broken and the imminent end to their beloved tale.

These flashes of real-life memories came and went in a blink of an eye.

'This cannot be real,' I whispered, spellbound by the whole episode.

I sat down to reflect. An ordinary boy would have cried for his parents about now, but not me. I learned how to stop my tears at home when they said my Grammie was too old to look after me. I stood up, determined to be brave.

'Let's see what happens next,' I said. I needed to find a way into the case. I swivelled it around, turned it upside down, and gave it a few hopeful twists.

I crouched down.

'Okay, little fella, you show me. What do we need to do?' I said, and the dog sloppily licked my thumb and then gently took my hand in his jaws, angling it towards the middle of the casing. 'You want me to... You want me to push it?' I whispered.

I placed my thumb in the centre of the golden emblem and it slowly started to dissolve. Gently melting away, forming a golden, slithering putty. The more I pushed the emblem, the stronger the tingling sensation became. The gold blob mass started softly creeping clear of my thumb, entwining around and through my fingers, across my open palm up to the glass hoop.

Shaking my hands frantically, I almost freaked out.

'I'm now seeing things,' I said to myself. I fumbled around to find the discarded scroll case in desperation for answers. It had unlatched itself on impact with the hard ground and was sitting there slightly ajar. There appeared to be ancient parchment paper, with old handwriting scrawled across its delicate surface.

I read it out aloud:

'My journey has drawn its last breath.
Sealed scroll opens only for the elected successor.
Destiny awaits.
Friendship and Adventure.
Fantasy and Mystery.
Good versus Villainy.
Seek the truth about loved ones lost
You are chosen, the new hope.'

There was a dark purple bag hidden behind it and another tiny torn note.

On closer inspection, it was a velvet marble bag, with a drawstring. Something you would see at a wizard's table. I opened it up and stared in.

Four glowing capsule-shaped objects about the size of my thumb were at the bottom. 'Incredible,' I said as the bright colours that were so radiant and alive began swirling around. Raging ruby red, cold crystal blue, lush exotic green and a black so black it cast a dark shadow around itself.

Each of these perfect little vials had a life of their own, bouncing colours back and forth like fireworks, empowered by a force overwhelming my imagination.

I put my hand in to choose, but one of these vibrant marbles 'the blue one' leapt forward like a magnet into my clutch, selecting itself for the task ahead like it knew what needed to be done.

In my hand, it felt fragile yet surging with energy, and grasping it, I felt an overwhelming urge to break it. Squeezing gently, it cracked like fibreglass, and I released it from my grip. The blue essence was now free from its prison, hovering in mid-air for a split-second defying gravity before spinning rapidly. Increasing in size creating a huge energy wind burst which surged around the room.

'What in the world?' I yelled.

A blue opaque spinning portal was in front of my eyes, and it opened up, revealing a shimmering transparent doorway with a gleaming rim. I could now see through to the other side, back into the room, but it was hazy like being underwater, and as I stared deeper, beyond it looked like a whirlpool effect.

'Wormhole!' I shouted. 'Amazing.'

My eyes lit up in amazement at the spectacle before me and then I remembered the tatty old note and gave it a read aloud to my audience of one.

'Oh, forgot one last affair as my adventure draws to a close. Hopefully, you may have met my faithful companion by now. Experience all the enchantment he will bring to your life. Use him to find my daughter.'

Abruptly ending, I was saddened not to get the whole story and it left me more confused. The note seemed to be missing some important parts, probably lost to the sands of time.

Stuffing the note and bag into my pocket, there was a moment of sadness which overcame me for the man who met his demise. I looked at the poor skeleton, but then looked down at my new dog. I could sense a new beginning.

I stepped boldly into the light with my new companion.

Chapter Three

'Okay, okaay, I'm awake,' I muttered only to find myself still on the settee in our living room with a blanket around me and an uneaten breakfast on the coffee table.

Was that a dream or a weird vision?

It felt so real that I could still feel chills down my spine.

I was back in the real world, a regular boy. No longer in a grave with a weird skeleton and a dog.

Thank goodness.

Chapter Four

After losing my fight with the rose bush and having that weird dream, I decided to brave the outside world. I met up with some of my friends at our usual hangout, which we did every week. My crazy sidekicks.

We had a rickety wooden fort which was built into an old tree.

'Mr Tree' is what we named it.

It was situated on the edge of Veilwood, hidden in a set of towering trees, nestled perfectly atop a hill ridge.

Once you dared to climb the free-swinging, slightly frayed rope ladder, your efforts were greeted with glorious views of the wide open. A hilly countryside as far as the eye could see. Here we had a bird's-eye view of the little sleepy mining town where we lived.

Though ancient, the treehouse was in good shape. A grand feat of woodmanship and engineering with a platform balcony, a small entry hall and a large room in which you could comfortably fit a full classroom of children. This little gem of a find was kept secret by our close-knit group to avoid other rival kids staking any claim.

I was always first to arrive as I liked to snag the best seat in the house. A comfy bean bag chair in a mishmash circle of anything upon which you could perch a bottom on. From deckchairs to three-legged stools, whatever they could drag from their parents' sheds. Also, I had a surprise for everyone.

'Looking good despite the spots,' I laughed, checking myself out in the small mirror we'd glued wonkily to the wall and running my hands through my slightly overgrown hair.

Being the 'self-elected' leader of this band of misfits, I always dressed to impress, making sure to look the part. Smart jeans and a quirky T-shirt with a clever slogan. This particular witty one 'Gravity: it's really getting me down' made me smile.

Next to arrive were the twins. Both blonde. Parker and Jessie. Brother and sister. Not identical and not the brightest pair. They constantly loved playing jokes on anyone on their radar.

Jessie being the oldest meant she always had bragging rights over her brother, and boy did he know it.

'Come on little brother,' she yelled as she climbed the ladder.

'Ya know, you're only two mints olda,' he garbled in reply as he scrambled up behind her.

Jessie greeted me with a beaming grin on her face like she had won a prize. Before I could wonder why, Parker's face appeared climbing over the edge sporting some new sun reflecting mouth metal, shining straight into my eyes.

'Wha ya fink?' he mumbled.

He was, of course, referring to the train tracks running across his teeth. It looked like he had them fitted recently and was taking some time to adjust.

'You'll finally have a model smile,' I replied. He grinned back trying desperately to slurp in the little dribble easing its way down his chin.

'Lil numm stil,' garbled Parker, as his blonde fringe fell over his eyes.

It was close to one in the afternoon, which was the designated meeting time, but peering over the huge drop below to see if anyone else was coming, I noticed Spencer, who was standing there staring at his watch.

'Oh dear, not again,' I said with a snigger. It was twelve-fifty-nine.

'Come on up Spencer,' I yelled down only for him to stand there silently for another minute before nodding to himself and making his way up.

'Hello Boo, lovely day for a get-together. Do you need any help with anything?' Spencer said. He continued before I could answer. 'I could tidy the den if you like. Did I tell you I got this new lovely stone for my rock collection?' he asked, flashing his amethyst cluster and proudly holding it up to the light.

'Alright, Spencer. So you made it okay? How long were you waiting down there?' I enquired, taking the cluster from his hand. 'Nice rock; it'll look good in your collection.'

'Oh, I was not waiting that long really, I arrived at twelve-fifty-three and well... you said one, so I only had to wait seven minutes,' Spencer replied.

'Okay great, so not long then?' I said, keeping a straight face. Spencer was one of the nicest, nerdiest, kindest kids I knew.

'Time waits for no man, so it must be a woman,' I said, making Spencer smile, which was funny in itself as Spencer rarely ever got my jokes.

'I'm here, I'm here,' came an excited screech from down under. 'It's me Benji.' He didn't need to announce himself. We all already knew who it was, with his distinctive loud voice and his excitable tone.

The boy never seemed to stay still. He bound up the ladder like a leaping gazelle in record time.

'What's the rush?' I said. Where he got all his energy, no one knew. He was also super smart, perpetually hungry and always had a story to tell. He was blind as a bat, and wore pairs of funky designer glasses, which he claimed made him 'distinguished and sophisticated'.

'Guess what happened in class yesterday?' Benji asked. Everyone leaned forward, wanting to hear the gossip.

'We were making edible dye pastes in science. Frankie thought it would be funny to take some and put it in the teachers' staffroom in a sauce bottle. You know grand old big brown beard, Mr Bigfoot?'

'He only put it all over his chips and actually ate it.'

Everyone giggled.

'But that's not even the funny part. For real. An hour later, we all sat in class and watched parts of his beard changing colour before our eyes. Absolute riot it was... and, of course, Frankie got detention again.

'Did I hear my name?' Frankie propelled onto the roof of the treehouse from a neighbouring tree. It was not the conventional type of entrance, but that was normal for Frankie.

The ever-so-boisterous Frankie was as mad as a hatter, loved a good argument, and was not too bad on the eyes if I do say so myself. With her fiery, wavy red hair, olive skin and emerald green piercing eyes, I never had the nerve to tell her as I knew I would probably receive a knuckle sandwich if I did.

She was my first friend when I arrived here. I still remember the day I told her that I missed my real parents. She took my hand and squeezed it, her eyes full of understanding. 'You'll be okay,' she said quietly, and somehow that simple line made me feel better, like I wasn't alone.

As we grew older, Frankie became feistier and more formidable. She was a force to be reckoned with. Having her around had its benefits; we got no trouble from bullies because they were all scared of her. Honestly, we were all a little intimidated by her too. But knowing she had our backs gave us a sense of safety and belonging.

'Alright, meatballs,' she laughed, addressing the group, 'what's cooking?'

'Nothing is cooking,' replied Spencer, 'were we supposed to bring food?'

'I've brought a snack,' blurted out Benji, unwrapping a banana sandwich and taking a monstrous bite.

'What the hell is in there? Banana? Ughhh, you say you're fussy, but good gracious, you'll eat anything if it's sandwiched in bread,' Frankie said, disgusted.

'I'm hungry. It was over an hour ago since lunch,' he said, stuffing in the last bite, still smiling.

Seconds later, he pulled an extremely odd face before leaning back and cranking like a catapult. Oh dear, something was coming. And then it came:

'Achooo.'

Like a bullet exploding out of a gun, a big wadge of banana flew out of his nose. In slow motion, everyone in the line of sight ducked left and then dived right for cover, except for Jessie, who had just sat down on her throne of choice. Before she could gasp or even blink, 'wham' a sticky, wet, juicy slap landed on her forehead.

'Bullseye,' shouted Parker, clapping away like a happy seal.

Luckily, she was calm and laughed it off. She could see Benji fumbling around for his glasses, which had fallen off in the explosion and kindly passed them to him.

'Good shot,' said Jessie, gently pinching his arm.

'What the heck,' chuckled Benji as his glasses slid off his nose. 'They must have gotten wider, or maybe my head has gotten smaller.'

'Probably your brain's got smaller,' laughed Parker, grinning again wildly.

'Wow, those are some proper metal gnashers. Don't go too near any magnets with those bad boys,' joked Frankie, 'Maybe we could finally have a TV up here and stick your head out the window for an antenna.'

'Lovely idea, but it won't work,' said Spencer, 'We have no electricity.'

'I have a joke about bad teeth coming, so brace yourselves,' giggled Jessie, trying to join in.

This could go on all day, so I thought I would stop the commotion. However, I couldn't resist making a perfect pun myself: 'Ahem, can everyone stop being 'bracist' so we can get back to business?'

'And what line of business is it today, then, Sir Spotty McSpot?' Parker smartly replied. I knew he was referring to my rather red polka-dotted body and face, and I could feel my face redden more. 'I hope you aren't contagious.'

Finally, after getting everyone settled down, I explained the story of my morning, and surprise, surprise, it didn't come as much of a shock to anyone, so I quickly moved on.

Sounding like a government official, I addressed my fellow citizens.

'Thanks all for coming to our weekly get-together, nice to see you all here,' I said, ignoring the moans and groans. Knowing I was losing their interest, I skipped to the fun part.

'Okay, okay, so on to the good stuff. Surprise!' unveiling my latest gadget. 'Got myself a toy BB gun. It's brand new, so who wants to come and make some targets in the field? We can shoot 'em down.'

'I'm up for it,' said Benji, who was always up for anything new.

'Good idea, but I am not supposed to play with guns,' interrupted Spencer, 'so I will happily watch for a bit.'

'I'll watch too. I'm off to kickboxing shortly,' said Frankie, who always seemed to have many classes to attend, most of which involved being active and mostly fighting.

The twins both stared at each other and lit up with excitement.

'Can I shoot him?'

'Can I shoot her?'

The words popped out of their mouths in unison, making us all laugh.

'Great, though no shooting each other please,' I said, quieting that idea, 'I promised Peter, if he let me take it out, no one would die today, though before we go, anything on anyone else's mind?'

'What's that smell?' Jessie piped up. 'Eww, it's so bad I think I can actually taste it.'

Parker held his hands up whilst giggling to himself.

We all climbed down from the treehouse, ignoring Parker.

'This will do,' I said, as we poured the cans all over the grass, 'let's get set up.'

This was my first airsoft BB rifle. Grammy told me that my real dad airsofted regularly on Sundays with his own guns. It was his hobby for years, and I knew I wanted to follow in his footsteps. Now I was finally old enough to have one of my own.

Airsoft is like playing pretend army but using lifelike replica guns at a specially designated battlefield with marshals to referee the scoring. Thrilling.

My gun was special, like in the movies. I had gone for something different, 'a classic,' an AK-47 like most evil henchmen carry with real wood-finish handles to look completely badass.

Getting it out of the case, I received an 'Ahhh' from most of the group as everyone put their grubby little fingers all over the sleek metal frame.

'Patience, everyone will get a turn,' I announced. 'Ladies first,' I whispered, trying to be polite as I passed the gun to Jessie.

'Am I not a lady?' said Frankie.

'Well, you do have a boy's name,' Parker bravely answered, putting on a pretend, deep, manly voice.

'Hey, I'm Frank, and I'll knock your lights out, so do what I say if you know what's good for ya.'

Frankie's face lit up with comical joy.

'Quite a good impression, little boy. I'm next then, and you can go last,' she said, stamping her claim on next in line despite earlier saying that she would watch.

Jessie half closed her eyes, praying to shoot something. She managed to hit three targets at close range but then got bored.

'Not much fun this, boys playing shooty shooty,' she sighed, unimpressed.

Passing the gun back to Frankie, she wandered off. Frankie immediately turned for revenge on poor Parker.

'You'd better run, meatball, I'll give you a ten-second head start,' she said as she flaughed (a special word I've made up for fake-laughing) loudly to herself like a crazy evil person.

He didn't know whether to run or cry, but I immediately took the gun from her.

'Friendly fire will not be tolerated,' I said, as I laid down the law.

Frankie was a bit of a loose cannon, unpredictable and had played airsoft before. She was well aware of the rules and those incriminating words she heard the last time they hauled her off for shooting her teammates.

'I didn't want to play your little gun games anyway. I've got some girls and boys who want a kickin',' she said as she stormed off to her kickboxing class.

'Goodbye, Frankie,' Spencer waved. 'Oh, she's not waving back, maybe she's upset. How disappointing.'

Benji and Parker were now taking turns spraying little white BBs down the field like speeding hailstones peppering everything except their intended targets. They made their own machine gun noises between them as they tried to better one another.

'Think it's wonky; it doesn't seem to shoot straight,' said Benji, miffed by his inaccuracy.

'Give me a go boy, and I'll show you how it's done,' I said confidently.

Grabbing the gun, I squeezed off a few light trigger pulls whilst zeroing the sights like a hawk on the cans of prey. Like the avid marksman I was. Ding. Ding. Ding.

Each careful, well-placed shot hit its intended target. I then stood back proudly to receive the rapturous applause, but it never came.

'Show off,' said Parker, picking at his brace.

'Don't let your head get too big,' Benji said.

'I'm not big-headed, my brain is overweight with greatness,' I barked, feeling good about myself. I smirked at the two of them.

The wind was now picking up. We all heard it creeping in, howling across the fields towards us.

It had been forecast for severe blustery gales in the late afternoon and there had even been a warning about staying safe indoors, however, does anyone ever pay attention to forecasts?

'High winds are on the news, they claim. How disappointing,' said Spencer, updating the group. 'So we got to stay safe. I reckon it may be more like a hurricane rather than a high wind.' He licked his finger and hoisted it skywards like he could predict the weather.

'If they really wanted us to stay safe,' said Benji, wittily adding, 'they should stop naming all these hurricanes after people's names, 'Gloria', 'Ian', hardly scary, is it? If they told you it was the ultimate killer storm V, then I'd have second thoughts about going out.'

'Maybe they should call it the Big Bad Wolf, who'll huff and puff and blow your house down,' I added, which received a round of chuckles.

Jessie, Parker and Benji departed for the safety and comfort of home to beat whatever force of nature was incoming.

I noticed Spencer still sitting quietly on a tree stump, like he was waiting to be dismissed from the naughty step. 'Guess you'll be off too,' I said to him.

'Do you need me to pick up all the white rabbit droppings?' he offered, as the airsoft BB pellets were now scattered and looked like a carpet of patchy snow in the grass. Unlike the rest, he always liked to help before disappearing.

'Nope, they are biodegradable, so no need; they disappear like magic.'

'There is no such thing as magic, silly. Okay, see you later,' he called out as he trundled homeward.

I was in no hurry at all. Sitting at home watching the square zombie box or being roped into family fun time playing 'bored games' was not my cup of tea, especially when George, the game destroyer, lurked at every corner.

I opted for a risky scenic detour home, crossing through some meadows left overgrown and abandoned, 'wilding' they called it, allowing nature to take back the land again.

The wind seemed to be picking up with every stride, and I thought maybe I should have gone back with the others.

The tall grass and vegetation were waving frantically as gusts of air bellowed louder, whistling past my ears like a cyclone.

The sky alarmingly darkened abruptly, and mist and gloom descended all around me. The now-hidden rayless sun caused a chill up my spine.

My eyes were now stinging with the wrath of daggers as debris was hurled towards me from seemingly every which way.

I was all alone in potential peril, and I was now feeling desperate to find a way to shelter or run to safety but had lost all sense of direction. My bearings had given up as I staggered, leaning into the boundless waves of the dark wind which engulfed my being.

The walk seemed endless, with my eyes closed and my face filled with determination, I faced the apocalypse head-on. I pushed through with every hope this nightmare would end.

The intense roar across my face was soothed by what seemed like murmurs of voices riding the waves crashing towards my ears.

Voices? Yes, I could hear voices. The further I delved, the more intense and clear they became.

'Chosen.'

'Path.'

'Chosen.'

'Hope.'

Repeating over and over in a ghostly pitch.

All of a sudden, the ground rumbled under my feet, and the earth trembled. The whole floor beneath my feet caved in, dropping me into the deep, dark below.

Was my dream a reality?

Chapter Five

Frozen in time and unable to move, my pupils twitched as the blue spinning vortex flew in front of my eyes. Paralysed by the beauty of the dancing light, the velocity felt like a big dipper. It gave me butterflies in my tummy as I travelled at unparalleled speeds.

Flash images of landmarks in our town whizzed by, as if the tunnels of this wormhole were shooting through station to station like a non-stop bullet train on a mission.

Then, I could feel my body relaxing, my fingers now twitching as blood was being pumped back into it.

'This is crazy,' I spluttered out.

Ahead, a blinding light appeared on the horizon.

'What the...?' before I could mutter the rest of the sentence, boom! Everything went black.

I forced my eyes open once the feeling of travel sickness subsided. My strange new surroundings greeted me. Thankfully, I was no longer stuck in a hole in the ground.

A whooshing sound came from behind me. Doing a complete one-eighty pivot on the spot, the strange dog launched forward out of the watery doorway straight into my arms.

Looking around and taking in my surroundings, the wormhole had deposited me back on the edge of the farmer's field where we had played earlier.

I was still trying to regain focus after the journey but was experiencing some unsettling side effects.

Flooding through my retinas was a landscape devoid of colour, and before me lay a desolate black-and-white version of our world. It was as if I was staring at an old vintage movie.

I was a little stunned and worried I had done some permanent damage to my vision.

It was difficult to determine the time of day, so I looked at my watch to check the hour. It appeared to be acting strangely, spinning backwards until it stopped at one o'clock, before returning to counting the seconds like normal.

Had I just witnessed the reversal of time?

'Wormholes and now time travel. Epic,' I said.

I had dreamt of this in a dream recently, and perhaps, thinking back, it did feel so real at the time that it may have been a premonition, but what am I? Some sort of oracle?

Something was coming through on my hoop, the 'Plane of Earth Astral' like its inscription was revealing my location.

'Oh, crikey, does this mean I'm dead?' I whispered, suddenly frightened.

I remembered just after one o'clock, we were in the farmer's field, so I ran back to the same spot. The whole squad was there again, playing and joking around as if it was only happening for the first time.

No one saw me approaching and it dawned on me that maybe they could not see me at all!

'Please see me. Please see me,' I repeated. Then I noticed I cast no shadow. My body started shaking. I was in shock.

Hearing my own voice was weird and sent shivers down my spine. 'Give me a go boys and I'll show you how it's done.' An overwhelming, sick feeling of disbelief covered me.

I was no longer me, standing in front of my double, trying to get his (or my) attention by waving and shouting. It was horrible.

'I'm here, can you not see me? Jake, Jaaaake,' The gun pointed straight towards me and before I could move, shots were fired.

I froze. Thankfully, the projectiles simply passed right through me, and all I could feel was a tingle as they penetrated through my phantom body.

'Oh God, I must be dead... trapped in the land of the living,' I whispered. My whisper was creepy, and I could hear the words echoing in my head.

The dog then barked, leapt out of my clutches, and started hoovering up all the white balls on the ground.

'They aren't for eating silly,' I yelled as he popped his head up like a meerkat, one ball still stuck in his nostril, while continuing to crunch them like hard-boiled sweets.

He was medium-sized, with a beautiful black and white striped coat, kind of tigerish, and a distinctive pattern around one side of his face, which made him really stand out.

Could this be the same dog I travelled with in my dreams?

'Why is this happening?' I muttered. Then I sat down, perplexed, wondering why I could see them, but they couldn't see me.

The real world and the astral plane combining together, but still much apart. Everyone said their goodbyes like before, and Spencer's infamous words rang through my ears like a church bell: 'No such thing as magic, silly.'

I had to make a choice to follow my own path, which I already knew was going to end badly or follow the others back into town. I selected the latter in the vein of hope for answers, so off my four-legged ball-crunching fiend and I dashed to catch up with my friends.

Warm, light grey beams of sunlight penetrated the clouds, and a gentle breeze swept across my cheeks—completely paradoxical to the horrifying wind I had witnessed.

'Typical. They said terrible weather, and it's bloody boiling and there's not a cloud in the sky,' Parker said, pulling off his jumper. 'What ya fink?'

'Did you know it's one of the only jobs in the world where they can get it wrong every single day and not be fired?' Benji answered as he pushed his red-rimmed glasses up his nose.

'That sounds like a good career move for me, then,' Jessie said delightedly, twirling her blonde hair around her finger.

'You know you have to understand a little about the weather. They do not let you guess,' Spencer barked at her. I could see the disappointment on her face, but no one else noticed. I never saw Jessie as the sensitive type.

'Got me there,' she said with an attempt at flaughter, 'I hate Geography anyways, and I'd be in a right mood every time it's raining.' I felt sorry for her as the squad wandered off.

'Guys wait for me,' I called out hopefully, but soon realised I was just wasting time, as they could not hear my cries from before so why would they now?

'How is this happening?'

In a panic, I sprinted as fast as I could to the one place where I could get help, and that was my home. I longed for their hugs and reassurance that everything would be okay.

Catching my breath on arrival at the gate I placed my hands on my knees. I was home. The door opened, and my pounding heart eased at the sight of my foster parents coming outside with the baby. 'Everything is going to be fine. They will see me.' They strolled down the drive towards me.

'No... no. This can't be happening.' I sobbed as they simply ghosted by me and moved towards the car without so much of a turn of the head.

Then, squirming to break free from his captors, baby George's gaze somehow met mine, and he began waving frantically at me. He became even more excited when he spotted the dog panting beside me.

'Boooo,' 'dooogie,' he blurted out in his baby words.

'You... you see me. You see me,' I managed to splutter out before Little G was expertly bundled into the straitjacket of a car seat and silenced with a dummy.

I felt a small ounce of relief that at least someone could see me, so maybe there was still hope, and I should not give up.

'You see, he wants a dog. Maybe next year when you are a bit older,' Joyce said. Then she focused on my foster Dad, 'Did you lock up? The door and the windows?'

'Yes dear, come on or we'll be late for the birthday party.'

'I can see the bathroom window open up there, you've left it open. Go and shut it,' she demanded.

'No time, love,' Dad launched himself into the driver's seat to escape. 'If a burglar can scale those walls and squeeze through our tiny porthole window, they deserve to rob us,' he said. She rolled her eyes.

I became desperate and put both my hands on the car window. Little G waved, but Joyce and Peter didn't flinch.

They drove off, leaving me in the dust.

I fell to my knees. At this point, I don't think I've ever felt more alone. Nothing made sense to me, and I was stuck in still greyscale. No one could see me.

'Whatever next?' I barked at the dog who barked back like it was a game. I reached out to give him a playful ruffle and the hoop on my wrist slid down a little, catching my attention.

I forgot about my hoop. I lifted up my arm, expecting more guidance or at least a sign, but there was nothing. The lifeless, useless trinket showed no life or help whatsoever.

'This is the lowest of the low,' I muttered.

We ran towards Grammy's house, I looked down at my new faithful companion, still happily along for the ride, without a care in the world.

'At least I have my new buddy,' I said, touching his ear.

Circling the last corner, Grammy's cosy little bungalow greeted me, but instead of being dull and colourless, there was an ambient orange glow to her habitat like it was on fire without the smoke or flames.

Charging myself through the door I shouted out,

'Grammy, are you home? It's me Boo.' Looking around, I saw no sign of life. Calling out into the emptiness, as I searched room to room. I eventually found her asleep beside the fire hidden behind a big armchair, her slippers snuggled around her feet.

I was about to wake her.

'She won't be able to hear or see you I'm afraid,' a strange voice called out as the dog's tail started waving passionately.

A middle-aged man stepped into the room with a green aura around him.

'Who the heck are you?' I said, even though I recognised the face from the old picture albums Grammy used to get out for bedtime stories. Her late husband, the adventurer who'd been missing for years!

I was little when it happened—his sudden disappearance. He had taught me how to make a bow and arrow from a stick and twine. I was a natural shot apparently. I remember how he used to call me special and say, 'You will go on to achieve phenomenal things, my boy.'

'Is that you... Grandad?' I muttered, not believing I would ever be saying those words out loud. My legs were shaking when I spotted his two small scars under his left eye, and I felt my heart pumping like it was going to jump from my chest. It was him.

'This isn't real. You cannot be here,' I said in shock.

'Indeed, Jake, it is me. To protect my family and keep hope alive, I've been living in a hidden world outside your realm. When I was gravely injured upon vanquishing my latest dark foe, I was transported back to the earth realm many years ago, sealing my final tomb until fate would decide it was time for a new hope successor.'

'But you look so young, you haven't aged at all,' I looked down at Grammy and could see she had as many wrinkles as the years she's lived through, 'and what are you talking about? This realm? New hope? And what about this foe?'

'Have faith and patience; things will become clear over time. I died a long time ago and do not have long left as my lifeforce in this spiritual greyzone is depleting before I'm shown my afterpath.'

'Spiritual greyzone? After what?'

'I summoned you to this spiritual, astral plane of protection, known as the greyzone, sitting between your reality and the unknown, where no harm can be bestowed upon living beings.'

'So, are you still alive?' I asked hopefully.

'Sadly, I did not make it on my final adventure and will soon pass on. When you found my body and my special companion, it unlocked my spirit after all these years. The Circle of Hope grants me fragments in time before I pass on.'

'Hope? But I'm not a Hope, I'm Jake Davenport,' I whispered.

Grandad gestured towards Grammy.

'My darling Constance was my hope; your mother, my daughter, was a Hope. In marrying your father, the name was lost over a generation, but you are still a direct descendant from the Hope dynasty, maybe not by name but certainly by blood rite.'

'Seriously I'm losing it,' I said, trying to make sense of it all, 'I'm talking to dead people. Things like this don't happen to me, I'm ordinary.'

'You are anything but ordinary. You survived a great deal. The Fire.

Grandad continued, 'You must have so many questions to which you will find your answers in time, but for now I will explain what little I can before I depart this lifetime. The 'Circle of Hope' is the life force for guarding the light in the living realms. Faithful knights, the 'Hopes of Light', are entrusted with helping those in need, solving mysteries, warding off the darkness and opposing evil, wherever it lurks. I see my darling already bestowed upon you one of the sacred artefacts of power, the 'Hoop of Hope'. He reached forward and took my arm in his hand for a closer look. 'This enchanted heirloom is a living, breathing entity, guiding its beholder on the path they have chosen, whether it be light or dark. Never allow this to fall into the wrong hands.'

His pace increased as he began to fade. 'Blessed objects of magical mythical gifts exist, but they are mostly hidden from the eyes of this world. Always stay in the light and do what you must to maintain order and balance between the realms.'

He persevered as his aura flickered and I freaked out that he might fade away before I got the whole story. I stayed quiet.

'Many knights are protecting the realms, and you are now appointed as one of them.' He pointed at the bag of marbles, 'Those are your travelling tools to help keep the universe in balance. Blue is gateway, green is time, red is home, black is death and white is life.'

'I don't have a white, I only have four. Jeez, have I lost one already? It's only been five minutes!' I blurted out, burying my whole head in the bag like an ostrich.

'Patience... you will see,' was his cryptic reply, 'They decide your quest. You control your fate. Always remember to fulfil your destiny. You were chosen not only due to your bloodline but also to your unique abilities to adapt and your resolute determination to solve anything standing in your way. The choice was easy.'

'Grandad, what happened to my parents?' I blurted out, my voice trembling. 'Did they perish in a fire?'

He looked at me with a mixture of sorrow and determination. 'Your parents are not dead my boy. I only know they faked their deaths in that fire to protect you. The darkness was closing in, and they had no other choice. They needed to keep you safe and hidden, away from the evil that was hunting our bloodline.'

'Faked their deaths?' I whispered, 'Why would they do that and not take me with them? And where are they now?' My heart sank like a lead weight to the bottom of the sea, drowning with emotion.

'They did it to ensure your safety, Boo. They went into hiding to continue their fight against the dark forces. Their whereabouts were kept a secret from all, even from me. They could still be out there,, trying to find a way to defeat the evil lurking once and for all,' Grandad placed a reassuring hand on my shoulder. 'They might be even closer than you think.'

My heart raced. 'Alive? Do you really think they could still be out there? Will I see them again?'

'I hope so,' Grandad Jack said. 'They were strong, resourceful, and determined. Just like you, Boo. Never stop looking, never stop hoping. The truth has a way of revealing itself in the most unexpected of ways.'

'But how do I find them?' I asked, desperate for guidance.

'Trust in your instincts, Jake,' he said, giving me a meaningful look. 'Use it wisely. There is more to their story, and the answers are out there waiting for you to uncover.'

'Last but not least, I'm saddened I will not be around to share more glorious adventures, but to pass on this faithful companion is a great honour.' He looked towards the dog.

Grandad stood up, teary-eyed, 'Patch is no ordinary pooch; every adventurer needs a trusted accomplice. He, although daft as daisies, will always be there no matter how muddy the waters get, so put your love and faith in him and you will cherish the rewards like I once did.'

'Patch,' I said calmly, 'nice to meet you properly.'

Patch quickly gave me his paw and barked, completing the change of ownership.

Turning back to Grandad, I saw a small, faint circle of light about to be extinguished from which I heard some fading words.

'Tell Constance I love her, and I never gave up hope. Good luck, my boy; you will need it.' A fleeting flicker followed, blown out like a candle. A deafening silence engulfed me.

Taking a moment of silence to pay respect to my granddad's passing gave me an overwhelming new sense of importance. I was determined to face each challenge head-on.

'To Boo and Patch, the great adventurers,' I said, looking at my new partner in crime, who, if I'm not mistaken, gave me a cheeky wink. 'Now, should we use one of these thingamajigs to get out of here?' I rummaged through the bag. A red capsule selected itself, 'If I remember right this should get us home.' I was right! A red wormhole opened like before and into the void we leapt without fear.

Chapter Six

Opening my eyes slowly with fingers crossed, I hoped normality would be gracing me with its presence.

I appeared to be standing in Grammy's living room, and she gave me a kick. She was relaxed in her armchair knitting, gazing up lovingly at me like nothing was out of the ordinary. I was amazed.

'I wondered when you would be chosen,' she said softly, 'I just didn't expect it to be so soon. Jack always said you were special.' A small tear rolled down her cheek like a single drop of rain.

'Grammy Constance, you wouldn't believe what happened,' I blurted out, but deep down I had a feeling she knew more than she ever let on as she seemed unmoved by the fact I had appeared from thin air.

Before I could continue, Whooooosh, incoming. Patch came flying into the room, but this time, no one was there to catch him. Unreal. He crash-landed onto the loose floor rug at top speed. Both of us watched in amusement as he slid past like a snow sledge scooting by, straight into the kitchen, crashing into the washing basket. Then he came trotting in like nothing had happened, with one of Grammy's brassieres hanging off his left ear.

'Oh Patch, I've missed you too,' she warmly greeted him as he went in for a big cuddle, 'you've always been a softie.' She untangled him, and I could tell he was pleased.

'Oh, my precious boy, I knew the time would come,' sighed Grammy, settling back into her comfy chair. I could see a twinkle of a tale or two in her eyes. Then she fell silent for a brief moment.

I took a deep breath and asked the one question I had been scared to know the answer to. 'Grammy, do you think my parents are still out there... somewhere? Grandad told me they faked their deaths to protect me. Are they still alive?'

Grammy's eyes softened, and a mixture of emotions played like a piano across her face. She seemed to look through me and into a distant box of thought, where painful memories and deep secrets were buried. 'Oh, Boo where to start? I had hoped that this day would never come; I've already lost my husband, my children, and now possibly you too,' she said, her voice trembling slightly, 'your parents loved you more than words can express. They would have moved heaven and earth to keep you safe. The fire... it was their way of ensuring you were hidden from any darkness that sought to destroy our family and preserve the bloodline. They made me promise never to say anything unless you were chosen, and sadly, that time seems to have come sooner than I would have liked.'

A tear finally escaped and traced a path down her cheek. 'I remember the night of the fire, Boo. After the flames had been extinguished, I went through the rubble, desperate to find anything that had survived. That's when I found the photograph and the glass hoop. They were untouched by the fire, almost as if they had been protected by a magical force. It felt like a sign, a message that their story wasn't over.'

I felt a lump in my throat, and my eyes stung with tears. 'So, they're really alive? They're out there somewhere, maybe waiting for the right time to come back?'

Grammy nodded, her expression a mixture of hope and sorrow. 'Yes, maybe, my dear. I've not heard from them since that day but never give up hope. Your parents are out there somewhere, fighting for the light and waiting for the day they can be reunited with you. Follow the clues, trust in your instincts, and you may find them. The truth is out there, waiting for you to uncover it.'

Her words hung in the air, a beacon of hope and a challenge. I squeezed her hands, feeling a renewed sense of purpose and determination. 'I won't give up, Grammy. I'll find them. I'll bring them back to us.'

Grammy smiled through her tears. 'I know you will, Boo. You have the heart of a true adventurer, just like your parents and your Grandad Jack. Remember, you are never alone. We are all with you, in spirit and in love.'

Leaning back, she made herself comfy again, 'Well, you are the chosen one now, Boo. Now go, you never know when the next chapter in your story will begin, but we two are the only ones from our family still here, and it is probably best to keep it a secret for our safety and theirs. If you must share it, choose only your truest of friends.'

I knew a bunch of misfits crazy enough to take on the universe with me, but should I involve them as this was supposed to be a secret? I was never good at keeping secrets, especially from my friends. I would never dream of going on an adventure without them.

Grammy pointed towards the exit, 'It's late, little Boo and dark outside. Your parents will probably be worried, so off you scoot. I will always be here with an open door.'

I checked out my watch, 'Oh dear!' It was eight pm, so I set off with Patch beside me. How was I going to explain being late? But most importantly, how would I convince them to keep Patch?

On arrival home, I tried creeping through the front door like a ninja, but no luck, Mum and Dad pounced on me like two angry bears.

'Where have you been, Mister?' Dad asked, 'Your Mum has been worried sick, we got back from the party, and you weren't home for dinner. When will you learn to leave a note or call us and tell us where you are?'

Mum, now seeing me in one piece calmly cut in, 'Just glad to know you are home safe and sound, Boo.'

Dad was still making a fuss, 'You're covered in dirt; where have you been, mister?'

I told them the truth, well most of it, up to magic bracelets and wormholes. 'So, I was rescued by a dog, and he saved me by finding a way out'

'What dog?' They both said simultaneously, as I stepped aside to reveal the hopeful new family member who had left a trail of mud across the hallway. Patch was putting on his best soppy eyes and whimpering like he knew how to win their love.

And it worked.

'Let's get both of you dirtballs washed up, and he can stay until someone comes to claim him. We will put some posters up around town to see if anyone comes forward,' said Mum, walking upstairs to run a bath.

I turned to Patch. 'Now you be on your best behaviour. If we're going to stick together there have to be a few ground rules, or they won't let me keep you.' He seemed to nod, gave a little gruff, and then galloped straight towards the sound of running water.

Before I could say, 'Wait,' I heard a scream from upstairs, and a steady flow of water cascaded down the stairs like a mini waterfall towards me. What a great start!

After all the chaos of getting ourselves clean and ready for bed, it was time to settle down for the night. My parents had made a makeshift little bed in the corner of my room out of an old futon cushion from the conservatory. As soon as the lights went out Patch leapt straight under my duvet. He probably thought he was protecting me or he wanted a cuddle.

'You sure do like your home comforts,' I whispered.

Wild thoughts were running through my mind now, and it was impossible to control my brain from exploding with all this newfound information and what the future may hold.

Am I ready for this? What adventures could await me and this strange dog? Would I meet this dark evil and would I find my real parents? As all the exciting questions scrambled through my thoughts, I knew I needed to rest as who knew what was in store for me tomorrow?

'Night night Patch,' I signed off for the evening.

Chapter Seven

The following day I rose with a spring in my step. There was no sign of Patch so panic set in. I made my way downstairs, edging towards the kitchen door.

My foster parents were sitting down at the table. George, the second sun, was calmly sitting in his baby chair and Patch... well he had been granted the head seat at the end of the table. He sat there proudly sporting a pleased look on his face.

King Patch and his royal servants!

It seemed like everyone was getting along fine. George launched some of his peanut butter toast towards Patch, and in a swift movement, Patch was collecting all the tasty morsels mid-flight with everyone cheering and clapping, encouraging more food to be thrown, and thrown it was.

'Very clever dog this one, acting human,' Mum said, spellbound.

'Listens, obeys and he even collected my slippers for me this morning,' agreed Dad, 'though my slippers are a bit soaked in slobber and now have a few extra holes in them. Guess my toes can breathe a little more easily,' he chuckled to himself.

I wolfed down my pancakes. Scrummy as always especially with extra cheese and chocolate spread and yes if you've never tried cheese and chocolate, it is an absolute treat, so be sure to ask your own personal food slaves to sort that out for you.

I was now eager to get out and show off my newfound companion to my friends and recruit them to my mission. I made my excuses and left the table, threw on some cool clothes (as I always do), and checked out the mirror.

'Come on, Patch. Let's go and meet the team,' I shouted whilst bolting out the door.

'Don't get in any trouble,' was faintly heard as we dashed out of the house and down the street.

Within minutes, I was at the bottom of the treehouse.

'I've got a surprise for you all,' I announced.

'Love surprises,' the twins said together, standing to attention and rubbing their hands with glee.

'Did your Mum bake her wonderful sweetbread again?' asked Benji, drooling at the thought.

'I'm pretty sure it is no one's birthday,' Spencer added.

'As long as it's not another pointless shooty shooty toy,' came a voice behind us. Frankie rocked up fashionably late.

'No, something more fun than you can wave a stick at,' I answered.

I whistled. Nothing. Everyone stared at me like I was a little bonkers. I whistled a little louder. Then we all heard heavy rustling and out sprang Patch, covered in leaves. He was proudly wagging his tail and had a large branch in his mouth.

'Meet Patch everybody!' I said, as he circled super excitedly around, dashing in between all our legs, nearly taking us all out in the process.

Everyone was quiet for the first time ever; their excited eyes lit up. We'd always wanted a mascot and now we had one.

'Livewire, like you,' joked Benji, pushing his latest blue frames up his nose, 'does he know any tricks?'

I wasn't even sure myself. 'Erm, I've no idea. We only got him yesterday and well, I say I got him... it's... a long story.'

'Rollover, play dead, lie down, paw,' came shouts of instructions from various members and without hesitation Patch gleefully played along, matching every word with his movements.

'I'm not sure he will be able to climb up this rope ladder. How disappointing for him,' said Spencer, swinging on it. 'I think we will need to build a pulley and bucket if he is going to be in our gang.'

'Impressive. Can he do anything cool? Go and grab something useful,' instructed Frankie, sarcastically thinking he was a dumb dog like most others.

Patch disappeared. He returned a few minutes later dragging something long and dangly behind him which looked like a giant grass snake, drawing nearer. We were all flabbergasted until we realised what he was hauling along.

'Oh, my word. He's only listened and found some rope. Did he understand what we truly wanted?' cried Parker, picking at his brace.

'I think we have an old plastic laundry basket with some handles at home, which would be perfect as a large bucket,' Jessie responded, leaving the party to fetch supplies.

I proceeded to tell everyone the story, starting with the crazy weather, being buried alive, and finding Patch, which everyone believed with open mouths up to a point. When I started talking about magic hoops, wormhole travel and dead Grandads, their eyes glazed over as if I was making it all up. Seeing their faces I didn't want to drop the P-bomb on them just yet, so I kept the information about my parents to myself even though it pained me not to share it. I didn't want to have loads of questions I could not yet provide answers to.

'Unbelievable,' gasped Benji, removing his glasses to clean them.

'Totally unbelievable,' Spencer snorted. 'It's not possible as it defies the laws of physics.'

It was obvious they were in complete denial.

Frankie was laughing it off too, 'Your stories get stranger by the day Boo, but I still love them all the same.'

'Well, I believe you,' Parker proudly said standing forward, 'You've never lied to us once, and a true friend always believes his friends no matter what they say, so I believe you.'

'Believe what?' Jessie queried whilst returning with a basket full of useful bits and bobs.

'Well, apparently Boo is a descendant from defenders of the galaxy and has superpowers, plus the dog is an immortal demi-daemon spirit protector or something,' laughed Parker.

'Plus, a magic bracelet, which acts as a flashlight and GPS,' added Frankie, grinning wildly.

'Oh, glad I asked then,' replied Jessie, blushing.

'I don't have superpowers,' I said, trying to defend myself from the teasing, 'Everything else is real, and I'll prove it. But before I show you, you guys need to promise this will be between us.'

Everyone nodded in turn as they silently agreed to the madness I was putting on their shoulders, so I pulled out the little magic travel bag and held it up for everyone to see: 'Prepare yourselves.'

I put my hand inside like a magician about to pull out a white rabbit. None of the magic balls put themselves forward to be selected this time around and I was left stranded, hand in a bag with an embarrassed look on my face.

'Nice bag of marbles,' Benji tried to take the edge off the redness descending upon me, 'my little sister has got one like it.' It didn't help save my red face.

Shaking the bag, I desperately delved my hand in again, trying to grab any of them, but they were escaping my grasp on purpose, not yet ready to play.

'You had us going for a minute,' Frankie said, half disappointed, 'I felt I could have played the warrior princess.' She karate chopped the air.

'Well, anyway, this dog lift isn't going to build itself,' I said, changing the subject as Spencer grabbed the rope and peered into the bucket.

'Good, I can work with this,' he said pulling out a boat pulley, hammer and nails, 'I am guessing Patch doesn't know how to build a rope system.'

Everyone got involved, and before long we were stepping back to wallow in our achievement. We'd built a fully working dog lift. It was awesome. Without hesitation, Patch hopped into the basket, took the rope in his jaws and hauled himself to the heavens. We all followed one by one and when I got inside the little monkey was already curled up on my beanbag.

'Good minds think alike,' I said, trying to squeeze in beside him.

Settling down from all the excitement, we were sitting in a circle. It was quite late, and we were all tired. Parker leaned behind himself to pull out his old acoustic guitar and started strumming some basic chords in a rhythmic pattern. At this point, his sister joined in with her unique husky singing voice which was always an absolute pleasure to the ears, and she even made up lyrics on the spot.

'Today..today.., was a lovely day.
I was with my friends, and this is what I'll say.
Boo..Boo.., what are we going to do?
We love your story, but surely it can't be true.
Patch..Patch.., welcome to our home.
Promised great adventure to the unknown.
Shame..shame.., we'd make a great team.
Wish your tale was real, sad it's only a dream.'

She was about to break into another line but was stopped in her tracks as a loud crackle followed by a flash of light interrupted her.

Looking down, the light was emitting from my glass hoop, swirling inside, revealing the words 'be ready'. Everyone lurched forward to get a closer look. They all clambered over one another as another crackle and a blinding flash appeared.

Everyone was speechless.

Taking control, I said, 'I did warn you guys!'

The sound of spinning marbles got louder and louder. Impatient, I put my hand in. The blue leapt into my hands.

A blue wormhole appeared and the treehouse rocked from side to side.

'Oh, crikey, who will join me?' I shouted out. Their faces were as white as ghosts at Halloween.

Too scared to move a muscle I left them and stepped inwards alone without hesitation, knowing it was my destiny. Patch was hot on my heels.

Chapter Eight

I emerged from the blue doorway, weightless, as if the world itself had exhaled me into existence. Below, an emerald sea of treetops stretched endlessly, rippling in the breeze. Above, the sky burned in hues of molten gold and deep salmon, casting an otherworldly glow. In the distance, a towering black mountain loomed, its jagged peaks slicing through the light, shadows shifting like restless spirits along its craggy slopes. The sun's reflection shimmered upon its obsidian surface, a stark contrast against the sky's warm embrace. It was breathtaking.

I was free-falling down to my demise. Tumbling, spinning with no control, spreading my arms out wide hoping to fly like a soaring eagle. The ground was fast approaching and I was trembling with fear.

I closed my eyes tight, then I felt a weird sensation of being cocooned in a soft, squelchy, warm embrace before slowly being pushed back upwards like jelly from a mould.

I was left lying on the grass, shell-shocked. The grass felt comfy soft, like a new mattress. I stood up. My body was shaking.

I could hear quiet barking, getting louder with every passing millisecond. It was Patch. He was falling like a plummeting asteroid towards the earth.

I could only muster looking through one eye, in case he was splattered into a pancake, but I was relieved when he made a dog-shaped pit in the ground. A few moments later, the indent was reforming itself, making squelchy, farty sounds as it pushed its unwanted intruder back to the surface.

Patch wasn't stunned or traumatised by any of it!

'Hey, it's you,' I said, smiling. He wagged his tail.

I looked around and realised we were in a clearing circle surrounded by tall trees. It seemed this place was purposely built as a landing pad for unsuspecting skydivers like ourselves, so maybe we weren't the first to land here and probably not the last.

Captivating red flowers covered the place. Each flower had three or four heads per plant. On one of the flowers, there was a giant butterfly lapping up nectar.

'I wish the others had come,' I said, wanting desperately to share this experience with my friends. 'They are missing this adventure.'

On closer inspection, I noticed the butterfly had three sets of dashingly colourful wings, and its body was so long that it could have been mistaken for a tropical bird.

As I approached, there was an uneasy tremble in the ground that sounded like a herd of stampeding horses. As the rumbling got more intense, I knew that something was approaching, and whatever it was, it was big and we had nowhere to hide.

Out of nowhere, a giant head snapped forward from the tree line. Its gaping, drooling mouth engulfed the poor, unsuspecting butterfly. Trotting forward, the rest of its large frame came into view. One could only describe it as a giant hairy buffalo, but with three menacing horns protruding from its face and a thick golden coat like a lion. Something was hanging around its neck, glistening and waving with each mammoth step.

I froze.

I didn't move an inch.

I waited and watched in fear, anticipating this huge creature's next move, but quickly Patch made a beeline for the heavy creature.

'Do you know this thing?' I asked.

I cautiously approached with baby steps and prepared for the worst. It was wearing a collar. B O B was carved crudely into it. How original. A Buffalo named Bob. Bob the Buffalo.

He didn't appear to be hostile, in fact, he seemed quite friendly. With a big, dumb, blank expression on his face, he elected to chew the red flowers. As I watched him from afar, red liquid poured out of his mouth.

Bob seemed to remember what he was here for. He bowed his head and went down on his knee, offering an invitation for me to climb aboard. His hair was tough and rugged. I hoisted myself onto his back, grabbing a tight hold as the great beast slowly turned to go back the way he came. Into the wilderness he plodded.

We entered a dark jungle. My little magical glass hoop vibrated, showing 'Laridia' across its glowing exterior.

I had never seen such a place on our maps. Bob was going so slowly that I huffed out loud, 'Can't we go any faster?' Patch, who had been running calmly alongside, understood my boredom and took it upon himself to do something about it. Patch pounced at one of Bob's two bushy tails and chomped down hard. The beast gave an almighty deafening shriek and set off like a drag car through the forest.

Boulders, fallen trees and anything in our path were smashed out of the way like a high-speed snowplough. Holding on tight, I looked back to see a patch-shaped kite waving frantically behind, holding on for dear life.

'Good work, Patch,' I shouted, watching him flapping wildly in the wind.

After a few more minutes at top buffalo speed, the darkness and density of the woodland got a little lighter and I could make out some footpaths branching off in all directions.

Hollers, whistles, and whooping calls could be heard amongst the trees. It sounded like monkeys hollering in the branches above. Except I didn't see any monkeys and had no idea what lay ahead.

Bob grunted away and pulled into a tiny clearing with a huge, sunlit, central tree stump. Then he clamped on the brakes, lurching me forward and hurling poor Patch up and over like a medieval trebuchet. He went headfirst into the canopy above, disappearing from sight. Bob then collapsed on the deck. He was out cold.

Hopping off, I looked around for any signs of life. It was peaceful and eerily quiet, as if the jungle seemed to hold its breath.

It was an oval-shaped stump; a centrepiece for something. Perfect for ritual sacrifice, so I was on high alert.

Suddenly, tiny pitapatting and whispers could be heard all around me, then out of the shadows, bright, yellow eyes appeared, blinking like fireflies in the darkness until there were so many, they looked like twinkling stars in the night sky.

My heart was pounding and a sickening feeling of dread covered me.

'Woof,' barked Patch from above. I could make out a large silhouette stepping forward and taking a leap from up high. The figure graciously glided to the floor, carrying Patch in his arms. It landed beside me and a roar of background chatter could be heard echoing through the surroundings.

Standing in front of me was a human-looking entity, the same build and structure as a human and similar in height, but with tough, grey-looking skin poking out of the makeshift fur clothing adorning the body.

Underarm wings, just like a flying squirrel or lizard, could be seen between the arms.

It was obvious these beings ate meat. Their jawline was elongated like a wolf's, and the sight was distressing. Two sets of big, sharp canines sat outside the mouth, and inside, there were lots of needle-like razor-sharp teeth, great for mincing anything unlucky enough to be in there.

I took a few steps back.

In my mind, I was thinking 'hairless grey flying werewolves'. Then it smiled with a giant grin stretching from ear to ear, showing off its pearly whites. Without hesitation, it stepped forward, speaking in a language I had never heard before.

He carefully placed Patch onto the ground. Noticing how gentle he seemed, I put my hand forward. He grabbed it tight and pulled me in close for a warm embrace. Then, out of every corner of this wooded area came the inhabitants—families of all shapes and sizes, coming to greet me. I was the new attraction.

Patch got excited. He did three backflips. Then he rolled over and showed off as some little toddler-likewerepeople were gathering around this energetic ball of fur, giggling with delight.

'You've made some new friends,' I said, soothed by the fact they seemed not to be a bunch of cannibals.

More cheering and whooping was heard, giving a feeling of joy and happiness amongst the gatherers as if they had been waiting for this moment for a long time. We seemed to be the cause of hysteria around the camp.

Moments later, I was hoisted up, held aloft and marched wildly along like I was crowd-surfing at a rock concert with absolutely no control over where I was being taken.

It was a shock to see some shrubbery and bushes arching over like some sort of trapdoor in the forest bed. What appeared to be a major tunnel, opening up from nowhere.

Chanting along merrily, they carried me down inside only for it to immediately break into lots of smaller pathway tunnels, leading in all directions, mirroring an ant's nest.

The walls seemed smooth and well-made. Light was provided by an intricate system of sunset-coloured gems. Pleasant aromas filled the air as spice and herbal scents reached my nostrils.

We were now going upwards and the tunnels looked to be hollowed out of the wooden trunks and as we rose there were doorways leading into living quarters, with many more spectators reaching out to touch me as I passed by their dwellings.

This intricate maze was like a metropolis built under and overground within the safety of these sturdy wooden structures; it was remarkable to think a whole tribe lived this way. Quite primitive compared to our own technology and way of life.

I pondered why I had been sent to this place, what these creatures would want of me, and would my parents be here, of all places? I was so desperate to see them again.

I guess I would find out soon enough.

Chapter Nine

'Welcome! Welcome!' Finally, some words I understood, albeit with a rough accent, bellowed out as we entered a large hall carved out of wood. Lowering me down, I was placed at the feet of a werelady wolf.

Looking up, I met her gaze. She was perched upon an oversized wooden sculpted throne. She was surrounded by petite older 'were lady wolves'.

'You smaller than last one,' she said in broken English as she raised her frail old arms covered in trinkets and bangles. 'You have to do,' she said, huffing at me. She ushered her guard detail out of the room. I was left alone with her and another slim male figure. He was younger and was adorned with lots of colourful decorations.

'My heir, Son, head house guard, name 'Lu-Ni' your guide be he,' she said, before beckoning him forward. 'Greetings, my hairy, pink-skinned neighbour from the Earth realm, welcome to the realm of Laridia,' Lu-Ni said with a sneaky smirk.

Then his face changed. He was now serious. 'Forgive the informalities of my mother, Queen Ha-Pe, with her limited knowledge of your language. Unfortunately, you have joined us at a dire time, so we need your help. We know you will help us as your father helped us not so long ago.'

'I think you mean my grandfather. My father was no traveller. He barely ever left the sofa. I'm Boo and the hairy thing, wherever he has gone, is Patch.'

Lu-Ni turned to me, 'So not the son of Jack Hope, the great knight come to solve the mystery plaguing our people and free us from our misery?'

'I am his grandson. This is my first mission, I'm a new recruit. I am the next chosen one apparently,' I said, explaining the story about how I ended up here and why they would not be seeing Grandad Jack again.

Lu-Ni placed his hands onto his face, gritting his teeth. He was saddened and worried that their 'great saviour' was nothing more than this inexperienced little boy with an 'itch' for adventure. I was it.

Their hopes relied on me and a four-legged creature who had trotted back into the room with two children still hanging off him. Heroes, we were not.

'Magic Dog,' the Queen squealed. A ray of hope had been ignited in the room. Clapping her hands frantically, she immediately started dishing out orders to her entourage.

'Feast,' Lu-Ni translated his mother's words into something I could understand, 'Hope you are hungry?'

I was. My tummy was rumbling.

'I can eat.' I played down the fact I was ravenous.

We were escorted back outside to the dark forest. It had been completely transformed into a celebration festival in our honour. Small fire pits were dotted throughout the forest. Flames flickered, spreading a warm orange radiance over the camp.

Hanging glowing ornaments of all shapes and colours were swinging from the branches. Singing wind chimes could be heard between the bashing of wood on wood, imitating the beats of a drum.

More and more gatherers joined, forming a circle around the stump, on beautifully handcrafted stools.

I was positioned at the table between Lu-Ni and Ha-Pe at the head with more than a couple of dozen important members of the community.

I had noticed a few spaces and empty seats, so maybe some late arrivals were still to come. Patch was granted a special pedestal to the Queen's side. He sat up proudly, licking his lips.

Ha-Pe raised her hands to the air, and instantly, silence fell across the community.

It felt like an eternity of calm discussions, followed by enthusiastic waving and pointing in my direction, whilst I squirmed in my seat, not understanding a single word.

Suddenly, everyone except the queen stood up, and a chorus of clapping and cheering began to break out. Was it over? Hopefully, it was over.

"Lu-Ni motioned for me to stand, and one by one the strangers took turns bowing and offering short, motivational speeches before sitting down again. I was the last one left standing beside my newly appointed guide

'You can say something now,' were his wonderful words of wisdom, putting me right on the spot. I was nervous doing speeches in front of my classmates. How was I supposed to do this in front of a big crowd?

'Ermm, thank you everyone for coming,' I muttered, completely unprepared, 'ermm, it is nice to meet you all, not entirely sure what I am supposed to be doing here. Hopefully, I will not be a complete embarrassment trying to help you. Hopefully, you will like me the way you liked my grandfather before me. My dog and I will try our best,' I said, giving them a weak smile as I tried to hide how much I was trembling inside.

The crowd, not understanding a single word, were left hanging in a limbo of uncomfortable silence. Lu-Ni addressed the congregation with some strong words in native Laridian. It sounded like a call to arms or an emotional speech to rally the troops. It brought inspiration and relief to his people once again. The forest echoed with the sounds of rejoicing and cheering.

Desperate for clarification I asked, 'Lu-Ni, what did you say to them?'

'I roughly translated what you had said,' he replied. Then he paused and repeated, 'roughly.'

'How roughly?' I queried.

'Well, I told them you are the descendant of the great Jack Hope, trained by the 'circle', have great powers, well-adventured and have promised to unravel the mystery, bringing peace to our nation again. They seemed to enjoy the story.'

'So, just a little roughly then!' I said, knowing the weight of the world, or at least this world, was now firmly on my shoulders, 'Is that all?'

'Well, not really,' he said, lowering his voice, 'as you can see there are a few people missing from our table. They and many other brave souls of our people have gone missing without a trace. Well, I said you vowed to investigate, find them and bring them home. Should be no problem for a chosen one.'

Sitting back, I sat there with my mouth wide open enough to fit in a football.

'Great,' said Lu-Ni, looking at me, 'you'll be able to fit a good portion inside there.' Food arrived on cue. They placed the food on the stumpy, grand table.

The buffet was extravagant and bountiful with meats of all kinds of animals, some looked familiar and some did not. Odd-shaped creatures amazed me, but the focal point was a ginormous cooked beef.

No, something bigger than a cow. A buffalo maybe.

An absolute vegan's dream! I thought as my mind drifted back to the mission. His tribe seemed to be depending on me, so I needed to bring my A game.

Everyone delved in, ripping and tearing slabs of cooked meat, gorging themselves like hungry pigs at a trough. Heavy breathing and grunting proceeded. All in a race with one another to devour the most, the quickest.

Patch, the well-behaved little pooch, seemed to go feral at the sight of the mountain of meat and was dragging some rib bones three times his body weight back to his eating spot.

What was happening? It felt as if kids had been let loose in a sweet shop. Mayhem! I retained my manners because I was well brought up. Carefully leaning over, I picked up a few small meaty morsels and delicately pried away some of the tender beef, placing it where a plate should have been.

This caught the attention of the wild pack of hyenas and everyone with their faces covered paused for a moment watching me gracefully popping in bite-sized pieces.

'Can someone please tell me where the salad is and do you have any fruit?' I asked jokingly, looking out at lots of blank faces.

'Salad?' Questioned Lu-Ni.

'Yes, you know other things that come from trees and plants,' I said, seemingly baffling him with my question.

'Oh, we wouldn't eat that. That is what food eats,' he said.

The chorus of meat-tearing and bone-crunching recommenced.

A moment of horror struck me whilst I was chewing on a tasty, juicy, succulent piece of meat. I remembered Bob from earlier, collapsing in a heap at this spot, and had not seen him since. Part of me wanted to believe he was okay, but the other part of me feared that I had just eaten yummy Bob surprise?

Then my attention fell upon a shadowy lump lurking at the back.

There was Bob safe and sound still sleeping off his recent jungle marathon. Phew, I could now polish off the rest without feeling guilty and on a full stomach. I knew we'd be ready to take on anything.

Chapter Ten

After the banquet, with our bellies bursting, we retired to a quiet private area to discuss what lay ahead.

'You speak our language?' Being the first question on my mind, as it seemed only he and his mother could understand me.

'Correct,' replied Lu-Ni, 'you are not the first to cross our paths. Jack also spent a lot of time here with us and I had the pleasure of being his guide. He told me about other worlds similar to ours and always had an adventure story to tell, bless his soul.' He then lowered his head.

After an awkward silence, he spoke again,

'Our history is a little primitive, and we are simple people.' He picked up a sharp flint and bashed it against another, making a spark to start a small fire, 'Jack told me, we are a little like your Stone Age people. Laridia is made up of lots of smaller tribes living off the lands, and there has not been war, only trade and peacefulness, since I was young.'

He pointed at his fellow clansmen who were passing by, 'We are the Shibok or grey tribe and have been at a truce with our neighbours since the tribal wars of yesteryear. However, peace is now under threat and potential conflict is on the horizon with the mysterious disappearance of people. Tribes are on a collision course, blaming one another for their warriors and hunters going missing,' Lu-Ni continued, looking concerned, 'we knew something was not right since the cursed mountain emerged. Everyone is now scared to go near its haunting heights, so we prayed to the circle and our call was answered.' He pointed directly at me as he spoke.

'You mean me, I'm the answer?' I spluttered out.

'Yes, you. And it will be you who will save our people. We have faith in the chosen,' said Lu-Ni, 'I wish I knew more, but it's all a mystery as to what could have happened to our people.'

I knew this mystery wasn't going to solve itself, so it was time to shake off the shock and put my big brain into action. First, I needed to understand what was happening.

'We need to go out with the warriors on a hunt. We can investigate if anything strange occurs,' I said.

Patch seemed to be nodding along to my plan or perhaps bobbing to a favourite tune in his head, who knows, but either way I took it as a sign we should venture forth into the unknown. First, we needed supplies.

Now what would an adventurer need in a strange place to survive in the wilderness? I thought.

Lu-Ni had already gone through the trouble of grabbing what he called 'essentials'

A makeshift leather carry holdall.
Two handmade hunting knives.
Cooked meat wrapped in leaves.
Fur blanket and animal hides.
Shiny precious stones and a rock totem.
A whistle-shaped instrument.
Little pots of various coloured gooey pastes.
Long stick with a menacing pointy end.

Pile of strange leather, vine and wood joined together.

It was as if my Mum had packed this bag for me. Seemingly a week's worth of stuff for only going out on a short day trip.

'Lu-Ni, are you sure I'm going to need all this?' I queried, looking at some of the other warriors preparing themselves in what looked like a fur nappy and brandishing a spear, 'I can't help but think I'm a little overpacking.'

I gave it a go and attempted a few strides with everything on my back. My knees trembled and gave way under the sheer weight as I toppled like a giant toy tower block, face planting into the ground.

'You may be right,' Lu-Ni said, quickly helping me up.

Now standing there barely able to breathe with so much hanging off my sweating, skinny frame. I was unable to move let alone run and was starting to think Lu-Ni hadn't been out much.

'Essentials only please,' I demanded.

Moments later, I was stripped back to the bare bones: Me, my wits, my trainers, my cunning canine and a few other things he still insisted I should take.

'Okay, now what are these for?' I queried.

Lu-Ni put a smaller rock totem on a piece of vine and tied it around my neck.

'Now you have safe passage through tribal lands,' he said, putting a small hunting knife in my pocket, 'for emergency,' and then got the little pots of goo.

'Red is for blood, green is for madness and blue is for poison,' he said. He was insistent, 'Remember there is danger around every corner in the wild so keep your eyes wide and your mouth closed.'

Now every hunter needs their tools. Lu-Ni began bringing out his armoury of bone-breaking, flesh-ripping, body-bludgeoning weapons of death and destruction. Long trident-like spears, curved swords with serrated edges and colossal clubs for crushing prey.

Wow and these are peaceful people, so I only could imagine what horrors await outside the comforts of the village. But this was not my way, I could barely lift them and anyway, I would prefer to use my mind as my weapon.

My forte skill was ranged weapons, so I asked, 'Do you have a bow and arrow or something to shoot with?'

For a moment, he seemed a little dejected. I had not opted for a mighty sword like a normal hero would. He handed me an antique slingshot. He then grabbed a small round soft fruit and placed it inside the leather.

'Now like this,' he said, lifting up his arms and twirling the contraption around his head picking up speed until a faint whirring could be heard, 'then release your arm in the direction you want to throw, before it hits maximum speed.'

'What happens at max speed?' I asked as the whirring grew louder, creating an ear-splitting screech. Lu-Ni, now struggling to control the spinning device, spluttered out, 'It either scares everything away for miles or attracts everything for miles,' his vibrating voice echoed back, before he released his arm, finally launching the object. 'See, like a rocket,' he yelled not watching or caring where the peachy projectile went.

Enraged bellowing could be heard from inside the camp. A mighty muscular were-monster fellow tribesman came stomping round the corner covered in sticky fruit juice all over his face.

I then took the reins and perfected a few practice shots of my own. I hit my intended target some way off like I was born to do this. Light, quick and nimble, I was ready to take on this new world without help from anyone else.

Chapter Eleven

'Love the name by the way,' I said, trying to be a little playful, 'and your mother must always be happy with a name like that!' I couldn't resist a little giggle to myself.

'Hold on, Jake,' Lu-Ni responded, 'Jack always laughed at our names too. I understand my mother is close to your word happy, but he never said what mine meant in your language. Please tell.'

I desperately tried to make up a quick white lie, 'Sure,' I paused for a moment, wondering if I should tell him that his name is Loony. I looked into his wide eyes and simply said, 'it is just another meaning for brave.' And we left it there - thank goodness.

The hunting teams Lu-Ni informed me were made up of five skilled warriors, so we selected our line-up.

Patch, the ferocious four-legged wild dog. Lu-Ni the skilful 'well-packed' Ninja. And there was I, the fleet-footed, silent, deadly-ranged assassin.

Who were we kidding? The three of us would struggle to take down a hamster; thankfully, two of the most notorious, fearless tribe hunters had been assigned to aid us in our quest from the queen's personal guard. I'll call them Scarface and Fruitface, as one looks to be sporting menacing battle scars across his cheeks, and the other was Lu-Ni's newly befriended fellow tribesman, boasting a nice fruity aroma.

Looking out into the wilderness, it was dark and gloomy with only a trickle of light from the moon's rays.

Off we dashed to face the danger, leaving behind the safety of the village and all those Laridians relying on our good fortune.

We were soon trekking through thick undergrowth. The light of home faded away in the distance.

The eerie silence of these wild woods was only broken by the occasional rustle of leaves and the distant call of unknown creatures. The forest felt alive, as if it were watching our every move.

As we moved deeper into the woods, an ethereal tune began to drift through the trees. The sound was almost hypnotic, a soft, lilting harmony that seemed to float on the breeze. I stopped in my tracks. The music wrapped around me like a warm blanket. The gentle melody echoed through the forest, reminding me of the lullabies my real mum used to sing. It brought back memories of feeling safe and loved, and I wished she was here. I closed my eyes for a moment, letting the music wash over me. It was a brief respite from the tension of our journey, a reminder of a time when life was simpler, and I felt my parents' comforting presence.

Lu-Ni noticed my pause and came up beside me. 'You okay, Boo?' he asked.

'Yeah,' I replied, opening my eyes and smiling at him. 'I just was... remembering something.'

We stumbled on into dark nothingness, with only a small amount of light coming from makeshift lanterns and my trusted hoop which had decided to lend a little faint glow to aid our cause. Scarface obviously knew where he was going, leading us forward.

The trees swayed in the creaking wind. It was picking up and the strangest of humming sounds could be heard approaching us. It appeared to be like a fire spreading through the treeline in our direction. Taking cover, our team looked nervous, even Patch had taken refuge.

'Shhh,' Lu-Ni instructed, pushing his hand downward, encouraging us to stay low.

The humming, now closer, transformed into a heavy buzzing as the creature was mere metres from our position, peeking carefully over the top. I could see a giant, flying insect hovering above the ground.

A firefly of sorts, but mutant-sized, with small fluttering wings beating so quickly, somehow keeping its oversized body suspended in the air. Menacing sets of raging red eyes were scanning the surrounding area in search of something, but scarier still were the flames flicking in and out of the mouth as if its tongue was on fire.

As it drew nearer, I could feel the heat of the air around me increase as trickles of sweat beaded on my brow. It headed directly towards us.

It was almost upon us when another unsuspecting, giant winged, flying insect attracted by the light came into view.

'Looks like we may have a fight on our hands now,' I whispered in Patch's ear.

The new invader circled above to attack. Without hesitation the firefly simply spat out a deadly accurate fireball taking down the insect to the ground below. This was no contest at all.

'Like a moth to a flame. Now that is what I call a proper 'Dragon Fly',' I muttered under my breath, not wishing to attract its attention.

I've never smelled a cooked insect before. That chargrilled stench will linger with me for a lifetime. The dragon firefly then approached its victim before wrapping its body tightly and devouring its meal from inside out.

Patch let out a quiet bark. Whilst it fed everyone crept out of their hiding place and made a quick getaway.

'What on earth was that?' I said, as I wiped my forehead dry.

'They are what you would call fire breathers. There are not many around anymore. Best to avoid if you do not want to be flame grilled'

'I'd prefer not to be a barbequed boy just yet. That was crazy scary, I'm still sweating like a snowman in summer,' I said, still shaking.

'I do not know what that means,' Lu-Ni replied, 'What's summer? And what's a snow...snowman? Anyway, it is best to make tracks just in case it fancies dessert.'

As we continued, we soon found what the hunters were looking for, and I could see Lu-Ni's eyes light up delightedly.

'This is exciting. Look, we've come across a 'Zeet', this is tasty and can feed a lot of hungry mouths, Lu-Ni explained.

'What is a Zeet?' I asked, looking around to see what or who he was talking about.

'It hops on two legs, very fluffy and has giant floppy ears,' he replied.

'Oh, like a bunny rabbit?' I asked half expecting him to know what I was talking about.

Lu-Ni became focused on the hunt, 'Good, it looks isolated away from its pack or we'd be in trouble as they are carnivorous, Gi-Li will flank around its back to cut it off and we'll try to attack the front.'

Lots of planning for a rabbit, I thought as I watched Gi-Li, formally known as Scarface, disappear into the darkness.

Zi-Qi gave a signal to attack.

'Charrrrrrrge,' I yelled, marching forward to glory, only to see this so-called rabbit up close and personal. 'Rabbit', it was more like a grizzly bear dressed in a rabbit costume, towering way above me, staring down with its enormous, glowing, sharp, white teeth.

'Nice big... big, calm... big, calm, sweet, bunny rabbit,' I said.

I took a teeny step back, snapping a twig underfoot, breaking the silence and chaos ensued. Not really sure who was the hunter and who was the prey at this point, we both startled one another and it luckily decided to bolt for freedom.

'Phew, that was close to rabbit boo stew,' I said relieved.

In one direction, Lu-Ni was covering the path, Zi-Qi the other, Gi-Li, waving his spear frantically, forced the giant pom-pom-tailed hopper back towards me head-on. Patch intervened before I was crushed, nipping at its heels, guiding it as if rounding up a stray sheep and wearing it down.

'Good save, Patch,' I shouted, seeing him professionally keeping the beast in the battle zone as Zi-Qi launched his fork-like spear spiralling through the air, penetrating its fluffy bottom, drawing first blood.

Oh, the excitement, adrenaline now kicking in, I knew it was time to do my part. Picking up a sharp flint-like rock and whizzing it, twirling around overhead, steadying my aim, but I was not quite quick enough.

Before the wind howls of the slingshot penetrated my senses, I managed to release, hopefully before waking up the entire forest. Striking a knock-out blow to this carnivorous foe and gleefully watching it fall, thudding to the floor, creating a mini earthquake in its wake.

Everyone gathered around.

Gi-Li pulled out a blade ready to land a deathly strike but presented to me for the honourable final kill.

'I'm sorry, I just can't do it,' I said, staring down at the wounded zeet, 'I like my meat, but eating and killing are miles apart.' I sort of felt sorry for the jumbo jumper, but this was nature and the tribe needed to eat. I passed the dagger back to Gi-Li, knowing that a hunting victory needs a yield from the hunt, but blood would not be on my hands.

The loud sound had attracted some unwelcome attention. I knew as I heard tremors and something or some things were incoming at a fast pace. Big, fluffy, pointed ears could be seen bouncing above the bushes and between the trees. There were at least a dozen more zeets coming to rescue their fallen kin.

It was an ambush. In fact, something out of nightmares. These were enormous maneaters and something told me they didn't enjoy eating carrots. The hunters had now become the hunted as we dispersed in all directions trying to escape this deadly duel.

I was twisting left and right between the trees. 'Thump' 'thump' 'thump' could be heard in hot pursuit. I hit a dead end. Trapped between two large stumps somehow entwined, I was at the mercy of my followers.

Turning to face them head-on, I found myself surrounded by a wall of fluff and teeth. My heart was pounding. Sweat poured from every orifice.

I closed my eyes. I heard some angry growling and snarling as Patch came to the rescue. He had positioned himself between us and was frantically pacing back and forth, warning off the attackers. The more he paced, the more deafening the growls became and his eyes seemed to glaze over as if some unworldly force was possessing him. His eyeballs glowed a scary, scarlet colour, warning off these vicious bunny bandits.

The baffled bunnies thought better of it and quickly hopped away leaving us in peace again. I was left trembling.

What was Patch capable of? I wondered as Lu-Ni came into view. We met up with the rest, unfortunately now empty-handed, but at least we were all still alive.

Daybreak was now fully upon us, and the failed hunt was over; it was time to return.

No dinner, no sign of missing people and to make it worse the mystery still unsolved.

Chapter Twelve

As we made our way back towards camp, a gloomy, cool mist and stormy clouds brought darkness and despair. We lowered our heads. No-one wanted to break the silence as we trudged back cold and wet.

Was this really the way back?

'Ziiiip', 'Ziiiip,' and again 'Ziiip', 'Ziiip'. Reverberations of insects whooshing past us like bullets in the opposite direction flashed past our ears. Building up to a steady cyclone of noise, joined by more critters and some smaller mammals wildly rushing by like schoolkids hearing the final school bell. Running for freedom.

Out of the blue, a spinning cloud of bugs headed our way like a mini tornado ripping through the forest. Without time to act, we were swarmed, covered head to toe in a wall of insects. We desperately tried to flee. Clearly something had spooked them.

Patch ducked to the floor, paws over his head to take refuge from the mayhem. I was not as quick to drop to the ground. The bugs got everywhere, in my mouth, ears, and I even felt some crawling inside my pants!

Last thing I remember seeing was our brave warriors swiping through the air manically at the tiny attackers. I shut my eyes tight to protect them from the onslaught of beasties biting and scratching away at our skin.

We couldn't just sit here and be eaten alive. I stood up bravely, swatting blindly, and tried to remove unwanted intruders from my clothing.

The horde, disturbed by frantic movement, eventually passed through. They dispersed into the wilderness behind us, and I opened my eyes again.

I leaned down to pick out the remaining bugs from Patch's fur.

After the insect invasion, we were greeted with a dense heavy fog as if someone was piping a smoke machine into the forest. Visibility was extremely limited and all sense of direction was at a loss. Barely seeing the outlined shapes of the rest of our party ahead, Patch and I tried our best to stay within reach.

'Helloooo,' I shouted, as they drifted out of sight. My voice echoed around me. Patch, still not leaving my side kept his ears alert to any danger.

Bellowing, flapping, and bone-chilling clicks, along with muffled screams, could be heard. Intense dragging sounds came from all around as if something was picking us off one by one. Kidnapping us into the wilderness.

Suddenly, Lu-Ni appeared on the ground in front of us. His eyes were wide and he looked terrified. He reached a hand in our direction muttering, 'Save me.' Before I could grip hold of him, he was pulled away sharply. Up and away into the foggy abyss.

Dark shadows could be seen through the impenetrable fog. Beating wings could be heard all around us. Immediately, dragons sprang to mind, but they are make-believe, and this was something very real.

They circled around a few more times, searching. A constant clicking could be heard. Fortunately, it seemed they were uninterested in the pair of us. They had a taste only for Laridian blood and we were not part of their conquest.

Eventually, these hidden winged demons gave up and returned to wherever they had come from. The fog slowly dissipated around us, following the creatures away as if it were part of their aura.

Looking around, we saw that Lu-Ni and his fellow tribesmen had vanished without a trace, leaving us all alone.

The forest birdcalls and ambient animal noises returned after all life had held its breath. Creeping up upon us with glints of light was the dawning of a new day.

Patch was wildly scurrying back and forth, nose to ground, picking up scents using his tracking skills to distinguish between our lost expedition and the way back to safety.

'You got the scent, Patch?' I asked and then looked him deep in the eyes, 'We could go back for help, or we can push on and try and unravel this mystery.'

Without hesitation or worry, Patch stood defiant. I knew he wanted to make a stand and find our lost tribespeople.

'Well, guess it's settled then,' I gulped, bravely clutching my slingshot tighter than ever.

Onwards we marched through the now-visible dense, green and brown forest landscape. We encountered all manner of strange-looking insects and unique, small animals going about their daily routine, ignoring the two alien intruders wading through their habitat.

We'd caught the attention of something colourful flashing in and out of the tree line, playing a round of hide and seek. Popping up in front, back again and into the hidden undergrowth, it dashed. Darting to the trees and around us with impeccable speed and grace, leaving a flickering flow of colour in its wake.

Patch loved chasing his tail, forgetting about his mission for a moment. This was a whole new level of excitement as he rushed around like a disco dog. He got bathed in tropical colour as each near catch eluded his jaws only to be covered in the pretty mist. Barking with absolute joy of the chase, suddenly this ball of colour barked back which bemused Patch, stopping him in his tracks.

'Patch, stop for a moment,' I said. A second later, I heard, 'Patch, stop for a moment.'

'Some sort of copycat,' I guessed.

'Some sort of copycat,' was repeated.

'Wow, like a parrot.'

'Wow, like a parrot.' Repeated again!

'Wonder what it is?' I whispered.

'Wonder what it is?' 'Wonder what it is?' 'Wonder what it is?' echoed around on repeat.

We stayed quiet and still. Nothing was repeated and the colourful creature boldly came into view, encouraging us to play some more.

If there were ever such things as fairies, this was probably the closest thing I had ever come across. Something between a hummingbird, a peacock and a bright butterfly mixed together and let loose in this world.

Utterly exquiseficent, is how I would describe this mesmerising creature, both exquisite and magnificent. I named it a 'sparklefly'.

Circling back and forth, doing loops in the air, and offering a mimic bark or two. It was trying to get Patch to catch it. A chase he gladly accepted. Watching him bounding around like a toddler chasing bubbles, I couldn't help but admire his determination and endless stamina.

'Patch, I know you are having lots of fun, but save some energy, so we can complete this mission and get back to our friends,' I called out, hoping he understood me.

Then I heard my words again twice. Another sparklefly came into view chirping away. It was followed by another and numerous others kept popping up all over the place, singing out my words.

We were completely surrounded by a sea of colour and noise. The repetitive chatter was overwhelming, as if we were in a children's playground.

I listened carefully, trying to hear various mimics. I was able to isolate and decipher some words, and I was surprised it was in our language and the voices sounded familiar.

'We're lost. Told you we should never have followed.'

'We're lost. Told you we should never have followed.'

'We are friends and friends stick together.'
'We are friends and friends stick together.'

'It's a trap, don't tread on iiiiiiit.'
'It's a trap, don't tread on iiiiiiit.'

'Arghhhh heeeeelp.'
'Arghhhh heeeeelp.'

'Get off me, leave us alone.'
'Get off me, leave us alone.'

'Where are you taking us?'
'Where are you taking us?'

Oh, my word, unless my ears were deceiving me, the voices sounded strangely like my friends, but could it really be? A warm feeling engulfed me, and I started to miss them.

'I'm hungry.'
'I'm hungry.'

'Was that Benji?' I whispered.

'Stop being a baby or I'll give you something to cry about.'
'Stop being a baby or I'll give you something to cry about.'

'Now that sounds like Frankie,' I half giggled to myself, whilst gathering my thoughts about how on earth I had heard that lot all the way out here. They must have braved up and hot-tailed it after me.

'Great!! Now we have two missions,' I said to Patch.

So, we need a new plan.

'Find friends, save friends, find tribe, save tribe, save the day. Simple dimple,' I explained to Patch.

Shooing the beautiful sparkle flies gently away, Patch and I had to find our friends. I realised that an adventure alone wasn't much fun after all. It would be easier with the whole team together.

Chapter Thirteen

Gathering my thoughts, I took stock of our situation.

Something was making people vanish. The Shibok were pinning their hopes on our success, Lu-Ni and our guides were taken in the night. My friends had been captured, and I needed to unravel the whole mystery.

I looked down at Patch, 'Just the two of us against this strange world, but sure we can do it together.' We continued on.

Every tree, every shrub, every flower looked the same. It was like an overgrown, never-ending maze. How anyone could navigate through could be anyone's guess.

Patch caught the scent. He was barking directions with authority and driving us forward with purpose and intent. I struggled to match his agility through the undergrowth.

'Slow down, little fella,' I begged, as wave after wave of vegetation lashed across my face as I tried to keep up.

I began to hatch a plan.

I stood a moment to catch a beat. Patch was looking at me with his head cocked to one side.

Suddenly, I heard twigs snap and ropes twang. It did not sound good. A split second later, I found myself dangling upside down in a tree, suspended by a vine trap, swinging back and forth. Looking down, I watched Patch sitting there staring up at me. He was bewildered at a Boo-pendulum, shaking his head each time I swung by.

'Another fine pickle,' I said.

It wasn't long before hunters from another tribe turned up. They poked me with sticks and spun me around. They engaged in angry chatter. I could only guess full with disappointment of not catching something a little meatier.

They looked like Shibok, but their skin was more of a dark, frog-like green.

I was hauled off, tied up and slung over the shoulders of one of them. Taken as a hostage.

'Where are you taking me?' I screamed, 'What have you done with my friends?' I tried to kick and wrestle myself free, but with their layers of muscle over yet more muscle, it was like a butterfly attacking a bull. I soon gave up.

Carrying me through the forest, I could see they did not possess the same flaps under their arms, instead they were sporting fins on their lower leg region.

During the journey to their camp, I was glad.

Patch had been overlooked by the tribe and was cunning enough to stay out of view whilst keeping us in clear sight. The little scamp seemed to be a pro.

'Well done, my little four-legged friend. They'll never catch you,' I muttered, with quiet praise.

We soon arrived at the edge of the forest, which then opened up into a plateau of velvety, green grass. Squinting my eyes because of the bright sun's rays, I could barely see a thing.

After a while, when I could see, it was clear a whole thriving village lay ahead. Tribespeople were going about their lives. A metropolis of various-sized wooden huts adorned the grassland, and smoke could be seen billowing from makeshift mud chimneys within them.

Dried fish and meat were draped over every nook and cranny. Animal pelts were drying out in the warm sun's embrace. On one side, there was a forest and a sprawling sea of water. On the other a skyscraper mountain loomed.

'Wow, picture perfect,' I said aloud, 'Untouched. Unspoilt by technology and modern life.' I had forgotten at this point that I was still a prisoner.

A deafening horn sounded. Then silence fell across the inhabitants as nosy eyes all peered in our direction. Armies of these sea-loving people left the water to see what tasty treasures may have been snared.

One look at me and life was put on hold, as its people rushed to inspect this odd pale-skinned 'not much to eat' creature. Pulling at my clothes and my hair, they gave me a full inspection. I was then paraded along the village for all to see.

'Where are you taking me?' I asked calmly, hoping for someone to understand and take some pity on me. We approached an open, central area, and the crowd size grew and grew the closer we got to the centre. With nowhere I could run, they put me down to walk the rest of this undignified journey.

For some reason, I was not scared; these seemed peaceful people, despite the same aggressive teeth and muscular builds. Draped in large fish hides, confidence remained high they would be friendlier than they looked or smelled.

As we went by a less well-maintained hut, I was greeted by a humdrum of excitement as I saw my friends in a holding cell peering out with disbelief in their eyes.

The whole gang was there!

'Don't worry I'm here to save you,' I cried out, stumbling over and landing on the deck. They watched as I was dragged along the ground, embarrassingly slowly, across their view.

'Looks like you're the one who may need saving, Meatball,' shouted out Frankie. It was lovely to hear her voice.

Not the best start of a rescue, I must admit, as I was slung at the feet of the chieftain, who was clad in what looked like scaly armour. He stared at me with ice-cold emotion for what felt like an age before addressing the gathering audience to decide my fate.

After much deliberation, something seemed to be agreed upon, and once again, I was hoisted to my feet, though this time I roared out, 'Wait, please wait!'

Sighs of disbelief fell over the crowd. With much hand gesturing, sound effects and body movements, it was as if I was getting through to them.

I explained my mission in a clear, confident voice. They listened well.

'And that is everything,' I said. I held my breath before I spoke again. 'You can let me go now and we'll get back to solving this mystery.' I expected to be free within moments.

The chieftain stood up, all of a sudden, and walked over to me, placing his hand gently on my head, turning me to face the crowd of chanting, green frog people. I dropped to my knees. This didn't feel like freedom. A sharp, curved bone knife was pressed firmly against my neck.

Was I being sacrificed in a ritual? I had seen sacrifices in movies to some higher power. The victims praying for a miracle.

'You're making a mistake,' I bellowed out, 'I'm here to save your people,' I screamed, fearing for my life at this point.

As I struggled, he held me tighter.

At that moment, something fell out of my tee-shirt, thudding onto the ground below. No one had noticed over the ritual chanting getting fiercer and louder. They were calling for blood. My blood.

The totem Lu-Ni gave me had fallen from my attire and was now in plain sight.

'Look, look,' I shouted, trying to point at it and get their attention, 'We have a travel totem, we are not your enemy.' Unfortunately, I wasn't getting through to anyone.

Raising his wielding hand aloft to the skies the final blow was coming to end my adventures. Seconds seemed like hours as I drew in my last breath. In the crowd, there was frantic commotion; something was forcing them apart, bounding in our direction.

Patch came dashing in to cause a disruption, rushing forward and leaping onto my back to yap aggressively at my executioner. What an entrance for my four-legged liberator and not a moment too late.

'Paaaaatch, you wonderful creature,' I screamed, finally hearing myself over my captors.

Nervous waves of babble erupted from all around the villagers and the bone-wielding bigwig lurched forward to grab my little party pooper. Patch leapt through his legs and ran off again with him in quick chase.

I then remembered the small hunting knife Lu-Ni had given me and I wriggled it free from my back pocket and cut my bindings under the cover of the mayhem unfolding with the dog chase in full flow.

'Shibok!' 'Shibok!' I cried out in desperation, holding the totem to the skies, hoping name-dropping may stave my demise. The bony dagger of doom was dropped to the floor, shattering as shockwaves ran through the village. The chieftain took an apologetic knee. He hung his head in shame, as I presented the totem at his feet.

Grasping the totem off me, he held it to the heavens and delivered the inscribed message to the now captivated audience. I didn't understand the language, but I did know it was a good sign when cheers of elation and celebration were reverberating in my eardrums.

The once tight, straight-faced chieftain was now overcome with joy. Even the bone-piercings through his nose looked like they were smiling.

'Shibok,' he said, pointing back to the forest from which we came. Then he gestured towards himself and his clan, 'Zaamuk,' before proceeding to open up his arms to the surroundings:

'La-Ri-Di-A'.

I got the feeling they'd not seen too many outsiders before and without a Lu-Ni to offer translation, this was going to be a bumpy ride as he pointed at me.

'Ti-Te,' he laughed, pushing a spear in my hand, pretending to kill an imaginary beast and putting a makeshift bone crown on my head. I was rubbish at charades.

'Hero,' I announced. He nodded.

'Ti-Te, Ti-Te,' he kept repeating as more and more joined in the chorus.

'Friends,' I shouted, trying to get my voice heard over the hero chants, pointing at the run-down hut where my closest companions were held against their will. Lots of head bobbing and shaking proceeded as he led me towards my friends.

Walking up to the door he simply pulled it open. No lock! No guard at the door! Nothing was keeping them there. I stopped dead in my tracks. It seemed they had been offered a place to stay rather than being his prisoners, which made me wonder why I was the one with my head on the chopping block and not them.

Chapter Fourteen

I stepped inside, taken aback by how different it was from the outside. The room was warm and inviting a far cry from the rough, unwelcoming exterior. Soft animal-skin beds lay scattered across the floor, and a grand banquet was arranged on a raised table, glistening under the dim light. The rich scent of barbecued fish mingled with the sweet, exotic tang of unfamiliar fruits, making my stomach grumble.

Benji was the first to speak, slipping off his designer glasses. 'Thought you were a goner out there,' he said, his voice quieter than usual. He wasn't his usual cocky self—just relieved, really, that I hadn't ended up as someone's gruesome trophy.

I raised an eyebrow. 'You seriously thought they...?'

'Can you blame us?' he interrupted, pointing around the room. 'Look at this place! Creepy masks, carved skulls on the walls. It felt like we'd walked straight into some ancient sacrifice pit.' He exhaled sharply. 'We figured they were keeping us here for something. We didn't want to find out what.'

Benji continued, rubbing the back of his neck. 'Sorry. If we'd known the door was open this whole time, we would've tried to get out. Maybe even looked for you.' He gave an awkward chuckle, wiping the sweat from his brow. 'I guess we let our paranoia get the best of us.'

'How did you find us?' Jessie piped up, nervously twirling her hair. 'We thought we were prisoners,' she admitted, avoiding my gaze. 'We weren't about to try the door and risk setting off some kind of trap or alerting them.' She shuddered. 'I mean, we had no idea what they wanted with us.'

I gave an account of what had happened upon leaving them all back in Littlehope, from my thrill ride of a journey to this point and how the mesmerising sparkle flies had led me to find them.

'Love 'em, those little birdie fings,' butted in Parker who was still struggling to pronounce his words with his braces, 'It was great telling them all the naughty words I could and listening to them repeat, total hoot. Until we got caught of course.'

Frankie then pushed him out of the way, 'Speaking of naughty words,' she said, smirking, 'Did the whole village call you a titty?'

I nodded, then quickly shook my head. 'I know, right? You couldn't make this stuff up!' I paused, then frowned. 'Wait... did you even know you didn't need saving? They just let you stay here! Like, how did that even happen? Last time I saw you guys, you were all standing around like a bunch of scared statues!'

'Benji, it was all Benji and his never leave a friend in need mumbo jumbo,' Jessie said, placing blame at Benji's feet.

'And I stand by my decision,' Benji muttered, defending himself.

'Yeah, easy to say now you aren't whining like a baby or complaining you are hungry every five minutes,' said Parker.

Frankie jumped in, 'Well, I'm sick and tired of all this weird fish they keep bringing us, trying to fatten us up for eating. I'd rather be hungry.'

'It's not bad,' Benji said as he picked up a slimy slice of inky black fish before wolfing it down his gullet whole, 'You know what it needs though? A couple of slices of bread.' He made me chuckle.

'Well, I was happy to go in the name of science once I got over the initial shock,' Spencer said defiantly, 'so into the unknown we plunged, defying the known laws of physics. I could not miss out, even if it killed me.'

'Yeah, and if Spencer says it's okay to go then we were all down from then on in. Except he failed to mention the 'even if it killed me' part back then,' chortled Parker, 'once we'd all got over the whole crazy wormhole-y fing-y, we all got frough just before it closed behind us.'

Benji led the way with the story 'We all then fell out of the sky. Falling miles before we hit the ground. We landed. Not dead. Happy about that, I was. Then we saw some little footprints, trainer prints and some proper monster hoof prints, so we decided to follow them.'

Parker interrupted, smiling, 'Oh yeah, we fought, you'd been eaten as your prints disappeared quite quickly.'

'For some reason we let Parker lead the way, an error of judgement thinking back, him not even knowing his left and rights,' interrupted Benji.

'I know my left and frights,' Parker said, holding his hands up, thumbs out, open palms towards his face, 'See the thumb looks like an L so that's left.'

'No right, silly,' Jessie snapped, helping him turn his hands around to make a pushing stance, 'Then you look for an L shape. You see, you had it the wrong way round.'

Parker then put his two pennies' worth in, 'So long story short we got lost, wandered for ages in the wild woods, got chased by all sorts of weird and wonderful wildlife, got distracted by those fabtastic playful birds and wham, walked into a booby trap and then ended up here. Captive.'

We all had ended up in the same spot, but experienced different journeys. I couldn't believe I had been reunited with my friends, here of all places, it was wonderful to see their beaming faces once again.

I slumped to the floor, taking a breather to gather my thoughts and felt relief we were together once again.

The old hut creaked with every step, the sound like a faint whisper. Dust clung to the air as I explored the room a little. I felt drawn to this place as if my mind was tugging at lost memories.

Patch was sniffing wildly at one corner, his nose darting back and forth.

'What is it boy?' I muttered, stepping closer to where Patch pawed at the floorboards. I knelt down to inspect, and with a little effort, I managed to pry it up, revealing a small hidden compartment under the floor.

Inside was a small box, weathered and worn. Carefully lifting it out, my hands trembled with excitement. Opening it up, my breath caught in my throat. A small silver locket lay nestled quietly, waiting for freedom. It was old and tarnished but seemed familiar - too familiar.

I flipped open the locket to reveal a tiny, faded photo inside. It was a woman not looking directly at the camera, her face half-hidden with a young boy in her arms, but there was something about her and my heart pounded.

I traced my fingers along the edges of the locket and my mind raced to my childhood memories. I could have sworn I'd seen this before. Maybe something my mother used to wear?

Suddenly, I had a flash vision of outstretched baby hands fondling the locket as it was around the neck of a young lady.

'I've seen this before,' I whispered, coming back to the present. Patch woofed softly, putting his paw in my hand.

'Boo..Boo..BOOO....' Benji shouted, waving frantically across my eyes.

I awoke.

'Thank the heavens' Benji continued, 'back with us are you? Gave us all a bit of a fright. Eyeballs all white like ghosts, bit scary, thought we'd lost you.'

Jessie hugged me tightly and said, 'So glad to see you are okay too, chosen one.' Everyone gathered round for a big group relief huddle, before releasing quickly because no one really hugs anymore, do they?

It got a little uncomfortable for Too Cool for School, hard-as-nails Frankie.

'Right, enough softie stuff, you got us into this pickle, so how you gonna get us home, Titty?' she said, looking at me for answers.

I played with the locket in my hands and noticed something inscribed on the back. A single word.

'Hope'

Taking a deep breath, I looked up at my friends.

'Guys, I'm afraid we won't be going home yet, and I have something important I need to share,' I said, with newfound optimism. I felt now was the right time.

Everyone turned to look at me, curiosity mixed with concern on their faces. 'Though you will think I've probably gone mad.'

'Well, mad hatter, I think this tea party is well past its bedtime already,' Frankie laughed. 'I don't know how deep this portal hole will go, so we are in for the ride. Let's hear it.'

'I need to tell you all about my real parents.'

Chapter Fifteen

'Your real parents are not alive Boo,' said Spencer, without thinking.

The room grew silent, and I could feel the weight of their attention on me, 'I've been thinking a lot about them lately. I always thought they were gone, but this adventure has made me realise that they could still be alive somewhere out there. Maybe they're even in this world.'

'Alive! How?' Parker blurted, picking at his braces with a bewildered look on his face.

'My grandad hinted that they may have faked their deaths to fulfil their duty to the light and left to... well to protect me,' I responded.

'Good ole grandad, throwing, oh by the way, your parents aren't dead into the ring on top of this pile of mayhem,' Frankie jested, 'but, seriously, how wild would it be if they are alive?'

Jessie's eyes widened. 'You think they might be here, in Laridia?'

'It's possible,' I said, feeling a mix of hope and embarrassment. 'We've seen so many incredible things. Who's to say they aren't alive and didn't end up here somehow?' I could hear how silly it sounded saying it out loud, but continued, 'I think... I think we need to be brave and keep looking. Not just for the answers to the mystery of this realm, but for them, too.'

Benji adjusted his glasses, a thoughtful look fell upon his face. 'So, you think finding them could be part of why we're here? If they are as good at hide and seek as we are at finding trouble, then I'm sure they are out there waiting for us to discover them.'

'Maybe,' I replied, feeling my face redden. 'Every clue, every strange encounter could be a step closer to finding them. I just have this feeling that we're on the right path.'

Frankie nodded. 'Well, if they're here, we'll find them. We're in this together, Boo.'

The supportive words from my friends gave me strength. I knew that with them by my side, I had a real chance at uncovering the truth about my parents. I held my head up high.

'So, what is the plan? I assume you have a plan,' Spencer questioned, breaking the heartfelt moment.

'Well, my last plan was to save you guys, although that didn't really go how I expected. We got there in the end,' I said with a small smile.

'So, no plan then?' Spencer bellowed out.

'Actually, I do have a plan,' I continued, standing a bit taller. 'We need to help these tribes and fulfil my destiny here. It's all connected, I'm sure of it. And once we've done that, we might find the answers about my parents too. It won't be easy, but we can do it together.'

I half expected a few huffs and puffs, but my posse of buddies had my back and now we were going to tackle this together, come what may.

'We will use Patch to help track wherever they went and see what we are up against. Then we can hatch a strategy,' I said, getting on with the task at hand.

Everyone went quiet. I laughed.

'I'll take it the silence means everyone is in agreement?'

Well, what choice did they all have? It was either go or stay with the local fishy people.

Some of the Zaamuk barged in, laden with trinkets, food and weapons to help aid us in our venture. We had their full support, though it seemed they would be sending us out alone as there was a lot of pointing and negative hand gesturing at the mountain in the distance. Could they really be too scared to join us going forth?

'Nice,' Frankie commented, rummaging through everything before picking up two identical short axes, each with razor-sharp crystal blades on one side and curved, long, piercing bones on the other, 'Can do some proper damage with these! So, I'm all set.' She stood up defiantly. Everyone gazed up at the flaming-haired barbarian as she casually slipped the havoc reapers into her belt.

'Well, the warrior role is fulfilled,' I jested, as the rest worked their way through the mound of loot to uncover what each one of them fancied.

Spencer had selected a long, gnarly, solid wooden stick. 'The journey may be a long one, so this will be lovely if there is lots of walking,' he said. As always, he had thought about practicality overlooking like a badass like the rest of us.

Jessie wasn't into holding a weapon either, as she didn't fancy bashing things to death, but she did have her beady eyes dead set on a carved flute-like device and a little leather pouch of darts decorated in vibrant, fluffy, colourful feathers.

It looked so pretty, she couldn't resist. Examining further, it looked like a musical instrument, but in fact was a blow gun. Loading an elegant dart inside one end, she raised it up to her puckered lips pretending for a trial fire.

Meanwhile, Parker had hit gold. Delving deep he had discovered some scale armour woven together with gold-fleshed fish scales. A real thing of beauty as he slung it over his torso.

'Little heavy and a little smelly, but I'll feel better knowing I'm protected,' he said, as he grabbed a trident spear of similar matching colour. It shimmered brightly in the sun which was beating down upon us.

'Poseidon Parker, are you there?' Benji cracked a joke whilst squinting heavily at the glowing figure before him.

Not inconspicuous I must admit, but whatever gave him courage to continue on.

Benji had really only one thing on his mind about this adventure; you could tell by his dedication and the way he licked his lips as he prepared his supplies. Most important of course was the supply of sustenance. He piled in as much meat and fish into a sling satchel as he could.

'A hungry army would be no army at all,' he said, before picking up a miniature three-pronged spike and a small dagger.

'Your personal knife and fork?' I laughed out loud looking at what now looked like an angry picnic protector.

Benji took off his glasses before he smartly replied, 'Not going to miss this, some of the best steak I've ever eaten. Did you know rich people eat more steak than poor people?'

'Why would rich people eat poor people?' Spencer asked - serious with his question.

Jessie cracked up and snorted, inadvertently releasing only the faintest flow of air through her lips. A small musical note could be heard as the dart inside, like a guided rocket launched from the other end directly at her brother. The flight path was on target, catching Parker's armour in the chest region before ricocheting up into the air above.

'Blimey sis, shaving it close, glad I was wearing this,' he yelled, as he bent down to pick up a feather which had fallen loose. The missing pointy projectile, failing to defy gravity for long, came hurtling back down at pace. We all froze in astonishment as the missile met its mark squarely in his left buttock.

'What? Why is everyone staring at me, have I got somefing on me?' Parker asked, twirling on the spot trying to see what was up before catching sight of his wiggling arse-dartboard, 'wha the?'

Then his lights went out, and out cold he was, somehow managing to stay perfectly frozen upright as if dipped in liquid nitrogen, the dart must have been laced with some paralysing venom.

As I approached, I noticed his eyes were still open, twitching, showing signs of life under the surface. Waving my hands across his eyes, 'Parker, are you in there? Parrrkerrrr!' No response came.

'What have I done?' cried out Jessie.

'How disappointing. You shot your brother,' Spencer offered an explanation.

'Sure isn't helping, Spencer,' I scolded him whilst I gave Jessie a reassuring hand on the shoulder to help calm her.

Frankie had already pulled out a blue permanent marker she had in her pocket which she must have been saving for perfect occasions like this.

'I never leave home without one of these. I'll make a little change,' she chuckled to herself, about to write something on his forehead.

'Don't you dare!' I warned her.

'No fun you, meatballs,' Frankie whined, pulling away slowly but still grinning to herself.

Now what to do? I was racking my brain as Patch approached carrying what looked like some of my kit from earlier and presented it forward, calmly showing the three pots of colours.

'Not really time for painting, little dog,' Frankie moaned, still upset that her own attempts at human art were foiled.

Then I remembered the guidance from Lu-Ni 'Red is for blood, green is for madness and blue is for poison, remember there is danger around every corner'.

Yes, this was it. Though who'd have thought the danger would be ourselves.

'Clever boy,' I said, patting Patch who was wagging his tail in appreciation.

Scooping out a little bit onto my hands, I could feel the blue goop tingling mysteriously and let off some quite pongy sulphur smell. Was he supposed to eat it?

I tried to push it into his mouth, jamming it in the small opening between his lips, only for it to sit there on his tongue, making his whole mouth look like he accidentally bit through his biro at school.

Patch offered up some acting for guidance as he approached a tree stump and rubbed his forehead back and forth.

'Ahh, I get it, like a rub.' I changed strategy, removing the clump from his mouth and smearing it across his brow as if applying warpaint. It did the trick as instantaneously there was a shudder of movement, and our friend slowly, but surely, was coming back to us.

'What ha ha happened?' murmured Parker sleepily, slumping to the ground beside us, 'And why does my mouth taste like rotten eggs?'

'You got a dart in your bottom,' Spencer said, saying it as it was.

Jessie came to apologise, 'Sorry little bro, that was an accident. I hope you're okay?'

'Awww, my butt feels a little sore,' he said, as he quickly pulled down the back part of his jeans to reveal one of his butt-cheeks. It was completely blue, 'I had a weird out of body experience and felt like something was crawling across my face.'

I investigated closer to make sure he was okay before turning to find the culprit.

'Frankiiieee,' I had been too late and although she failed to write on his head, she did have plenty of time to sneakily draw a fancy curly handlebar moustache on the poor kid.

'Makes him look distinguished and takes the focus off the braces,' she cheekily replied. Poor Parker blue mouth, face, bum and now he was sporting a fetching blue tache.

What a nightmare bunch we were, we couldn't even get ourselves ready properly let alone take on the world.

Chapter Sixteen

'Time to bid our farewells,' I announced to the group as we began rounding up all our gear. I exited the hut to receive a loud, rapturous applause like astronauts being sent off on a mission to the unknown.

'Farewell, farewell, farewell,' Spencer repeated, giving a little robotic wave to each Zaamuk he passed by.

'You don't need to say it to absolutely everyone,' Benji laughed, the crowd growing louder and bigger each time one of us appeared in the open, 'Wow, what a proper send-off.'

'Time to blow this joint, meatballs,' Frankie said, holding her arms up high, 'Hurry up Jessie! We need to make tracks and oh yeah and you can come too, my little Boy Blue.'

'Fanks. Fanks for everything,' Parker said, leaving the hut while waving at the adoring fans. Last out was Jessie, who nervously gave a little curtsy, overwhelmed by the mob of well-wishers. She followed behind us quietly.

'And thanks for not decapitating me in front of my friends,' I shouted, knowing full well they didn't understand what I was saying.

'Yes, it was rather splendid that you did not lose your head. That would not have been nice to watch,' Spencer replied.

All of us laughed, and my flock was ready for the flight to freedom.

The Zaamuk cleared a path for us, and we made a beeline for the other side of the village, Patch leading the way.

'Are you sure Patch?' I asked as we reached the water's edge. He dipped his paws in the icy, cool, turquoise water and sniffed the air, seemingly undeterred by the fact that we'd run out of dry land.

'I'm not swimming through,' Benji said, turning his back to the village. Hundreds of pairs of eyes were still observing our heroic departure, 'I'm not going back there either.'

Fortunately, a few younger Zaamuk children playing in the water saw our dilemma and pointed towards what appeared to be a black, spotted carcass of a large mammal, gutted and hollowed out on the shoreline.

'We have ourselves a boat,' I proudly declared.

'That is not a boat,' Spencer corrected. 'It looks like a dead whale.'

'Whale, boat... whatever,' Frankie said as she attempted a whaleboat launch single-handed, 'Come on, you lot! Put your back into it and help me get this in the water!'

Quick as a flash, we worked together, and soon enough we were all sitting in the whaleboat, floating away from shore with the tribe's frantic jubilation fading behind us.

'How do we steer?' Jessie questioned as Parker pulled some stiff, dried fish tails from under his feet.

'Foars – Fish Oars' he replied, as he dipped them into the water to start rowing, 'Which way, guvnor?' looking for guidance from our four-legged navigator.

Patch understood and took the helm, guiding us forth, pointing a paw towards the emerging mountain.

'I don't feel so good,' Benji whimpered, his face turning from white to a sickly shade of goblin green. His hand gripped his stomach and I knew that he was full of sea sickness.

'Told you not to eat all the foreign food,' Frankie scolded him, as he lost his lunch, turning the water green.

'Wonder what this used to be when it was alive?' I enquired, noting the legs underneath and around the head of our makeshift boat, there were also fluffy, gill-like bristles in the wind.

'Looks like an axolotl,' Spencer said.

'An axe-a-what-all?' I replied.

'Axolotls are a type of salamander lizard which lives underwater. I have one at home; surely you guys have seen him at my house?' Spencer said.

'You mean the weird alien-looking pink fish with legs?' Benji said. Spencer's parents were never too keen on visitors, so we never went to Spencer's home. Plus, he lived the furthest away, an extra five-minute walk, which to us might as well have been another planet.

'Called him Gulpy. Not a fish nor an alien,' Spencer said, 'Super cute and always hungry. They should only grow to about a foot long. They make great pets. Come in all sorts of colours.'

Benji, now pale as a ghost, watched a shoal of little fish munching pieces of his last meal at the water's surface. He then noticed a large dark shadow looming beneath the water.

'Ermm, are they carnivores?' he asked, wading in on the conversation.

'No,' Spencer countered.

'Phew,' Benji seemed relieved.

Spencer hadn't quite finished.

'They will eat absolutely anything, mine will even eat stones at the bottom of the tank, ferocious little monsters.'

Benji quickly pulled back into the boat, 'Then we may have a problem as I think there is one out there a little longer than a foot.'

All of us lurched over to the side, half-capsizing our raft. Sure enough, a behemoth outline could be seen circling below the surface, much larger than our floating corpse. I felt uneasy and stayed perfectly still. When I glanced around the others they were doing exactly the same thing.

Spencer, being Spencer, continued without much thought, 'They will even eat each other if you put two different sizes in a tank. No teeth. They simply swallow everything whole.' Then he drew breath about to continue with more frightening facts. I had to stop him talking. 'Spencer, not the time nor the place,' I said through clenched teeth. The shadow lurked beneath and seemed to grow as it came up to investigate.

'Row, like our lives depend on it!' I shouted as everyone grabbed whatever they could to help propel us faster towards land. My heart was pounding! We were close. Safety was within spitting distance!

'Think it may have got bored and given up,' Parker said, easing up slightly as the axa-boat-al ran aground in the muddy embankment.

Hopping out one by one, we were relieved we were on dry land.

'Close one,' Parker and Jessie said, looking at each other. 'Snap,' they laughed together as if nothing had happened.

'Not so tough now,' Benji bravely barked back at the now still, silent waters.

'Guys, probably best to move as one more thing...' Spencer said, hurrying away.

'No more things, Spencer. Stop the scary facts and be quiet. We are fine now,' Frankie snapped back at him.

I just about caught the next line Spencer muttered, 'They are amphibians. They can breathe out of water'

Just a split-second later, a rip-roaring rogue wave approached like a mini tsunami on a direct collision course. With no time to move, it struck the bank with violent force, wiping us all off our feet, pushing us a little further inland as water engulfed us.

A daunting, slurping sound could be heard behind us. A mutant alien looking, bus-sized creature emerged, swallowing our previous mode of transport with poor Patch still on board.

'Patch,' I screamed as the waters started receding, dragging my soul towards the toothless hoover of horror. I splashed around desperately trying not to be consumed like Patch, but the water suction was too strong to swim away. I was inching closer to my demise, on course to join the tail-wagger in the belly of the beast.

Frankie shouted out, 'Here, Boo, use this spear-a-lotl,' as she placed Parker's gold trident into my hands.

Jumping up out of the water like a dolphin, I launched the golden weapon forward striking my foe square on the nose. Ear-piercing shrieks could be heard as the creature rebounded back to the water, leaving a trail of blood in its wake.

The red water was left still and lifeless, and seconds felt like hours. Our dangerous encounter may have been over, but it had taken our smallest adventurer. I was completely overcome with sadness and guilt. I had not dived in to save Patch.

Benji tried to console me, 'Really sorry, Boo, I know what he meant to you.' We all sat down to take a moment to mourn our loss whilst Frankie dried out our wet clothes.

'It's not really adventures of Boo and Patch anymore, it's more like Boo and friends now,' Frankie said, trying to make light of the situation. 'We should complete this adventure together in his memory.'

'Fought he was some super cosmic dog?' Parker said, 'You can't have a hero dog and he dies at the first sign of danger, what type of hero would that be?'

'Quiet, Parker,' his sister scolded, but it was true, the pup had survived many great adventures, and then one day with me, it was game over. I lost both my parents and now I'd lost my dog.

'I think they may have chosen the wrong hope,' I whispered.

Spencer was at the water's edge I guess he was trying to study the diversity of nature after seeing a giant version of his beloved pet.

'It seems over time in this world without the plague of humankind, life has thrived. New species and the old have been able to evolve without interference,' he bumbled, gazing in amazement over the teeming life of birds, insects and animals around the water's edge thinking of what wonders were yet to be uncovered.

'Alright Attenborough, enough daydreaming, get your head in the game,' Frankie said, yanking him back to join the gang, and as she did, bubbling could be heard, 'Is that you letting a sneaky one out?' Frankie asked, trying to make light of the situation. She found humour the best way to deal with issues like loss.

'No, I did not break wind,' said Spencer.

We all peered across the sun's watery reflection where a melody of bubbles was breaking to the surface.

'Something is happening,' Benji called out, with his knife and fork at the ready for a fight. We all stood to attention like meerkats rapidly moving from side to side on high alert.

What peril would be punishing us next?

Then a large bubble erupted to the surface, cannonballing a soggy ball of fluff up high, eclipsing the sun and back down into the muddy earth beside us.

'Hero dog?' Parker asked hopefully, as I rushed to investigate.

It was him, my beloved companion, but something was wrong. He just lay there, lifeless, covered head to toe with stomach slime. Everyone crowded around.

'I know CPR,' I announced, pushing everyone out of the way to try and wrestle the life back into this little scamp. 'Mouth-to-mouth isn't working,' I cried, as I lifted my head with mucus dripping from my chin.

Jessie and Parker turned away, not able to watch. Benji was listening for a heartbeat with his head on Patch's chest as I tried my best again to revive him.

'He's gone,' Benji said, raising his head after wiping goop from his glasses.

'Don't you have a magic spell or something?' Spencer asked.

'He's not Merlin the blimmin' wizard,' Frankie snapped.

I stood up, 'No, maybe he's right,' as I felt a new sense of power emanating through my body. Peering into my tool bag, I was delighted to find that the capsules had magically multiplied. The 'missing white one, which meant life' was now there, clear as day. So white, its reflective surface gave a mirror image of my face as I looked in.

I wasn't missing a capsule; it was hidden until it was needed. Without a moment's hesitation, I put my hand in and it popped out on cue.

Holding the capsule above Patch's corpse, everyone took a step back as I crushed the glass. A stinging beam of light shone out in all directions like a supernova before collapsing back on itself with a loud thunder crack, burning up in my grasp. The ashes fell like glistening snowflakes gently. Penetrating into the lifeless body below.

A bright glow radiated from Patch, with sparkling bolts flashing through his veins. An invisible force lifted his limp frame above our heads as if being beamed up by a UFO.

'I think something is happening, Merlin,' Benji said, looking smug as Frankie ate her own words.

'Sshhh!' I begged, watching and praying that the light was not the doors of heaven taking his brave soul.

A glowing image of Patch's heart was projected out before us and we could see clearly there was no pulse, no life. A series of glowing vein highways could be seen punching through the organ walls. Electric bursts like a defibrillator lit up the air, igniting his heart and giving life back to our faithful companion.

The unknown force carefully placed Patch to the ground at our feet and the magical light display slowly washed away on the wind.

Chapter Seventeen

Had we resurrected the dead? 'Is it working?' Parker asked, keeping his fingers crossed. My heart was pounding.

'Give it a minute,' said Jessie, jumping in.

An eye opened from our fallen friend, then a slight movement of his tail. Finally, he let out a deep breath, and his tongue came out panting.

'You're alive,' I rejoiced, reaching down to embrace my little treasure. Jumping up like a jack rabbit, he was back. Bounding around us, spinning wildly with excitement like a newborn puppy.

'Never doubted it for a minute,' Benji said, and we all chuckled.

'Can we get moving now?' Frankie pleaded. We gathered our wits and gear and headed out again, following our born-again guide.

'Everyone got everything?' I asked.

'Well, not me,' said Parker, kicking at his trainers, 'Frankie and you chucked my weapon into the water.'

'I'll chuck you in the water,' Frankie replied.

'Do not worry, Parker, you can have mine for a bit,' said Spencer, handing his stick to him.

'Now you can at least play fetch,' Jessie said, in jest.

We were back in good spirits but still had some way to go and nightfall was fast approaching. Wild fields lay ahead as far as the eye could see. A minefield through super-sharp, thorny bushes would be our path. Boggy underfoot, making the journey both treacherous and energy-zapping, as we trudged along.

'Don't like the look of these spiny thorns,' Frankie moaned, chopping us a path through, 'Be careful, it seems everything wants to eat, sting or poison us.'

'Seems we are losing the light,' I said, 'best we find somewhere to take refuge as I've seen some of the nightmares of the night.' A spine-tingling shudder rose up my back.

Patch was one step ahead. He darted off. Was he searching for a safe haven? He returned two minutes later with a gratified look upon his face.

'Found something, boy?' I asked. We all followed him along under a dusky pink sky. We had reached our destination for the night. A small cave dwelling burrowed uninvitingly at the base of a spooky tree with gangly limbs, weather-beaten and oddly reminiscent of a face.

'Nothing cries safety like the tree from nightmares,' Benji said, looking up and down before adjusting his glasses.

I tried to calm the group, 'Whatever it was is probably long gone and we have a place for shelter. If Patch chose it then I'm sure it will be fine.'

We all settled in for the night. It was chilly and we all shivered. Gathering up some fallen wood, the twins tried to get a fire going, 'Not working,' Parker said, giving up after numerous failed attempts at rubbing some sticks together and clicking some pebbles hoping for sparks.

'Here are some matches, meatball,' Frankie said, passing them on.

'You had these the whole time? And why do you have them?' Jessie cried out.

'Yeah, because... and you're welcome,' she said.

Our little campfire was now alight and giving off much-needed warmth, battling the pitch-blackness. We took turns keeping watch whilst the others tried to get some shut-eye.

Spencer was soon sound asleep, but no one else was able to get any winks with the rustling of leaves, creaking branches, and nighttime animal sounds heightening our senses and fraying our nerves.

'You know, Boo, sometimes the answers we're looking for are right in front of us. We just need to be brave enough to see them,' Jessie said.

'Yeah, bravery.' I said, nodding, thinking about my parents. I knew finding my parents may mean facing the unknown with courage.

It was my turn to take watch as the others huddled together in a vain attempt at rest. As I gazed up at the stars above, Patch lay across my lap. I noticed the moon and night sky looked different here. Yes, it resembled our moon, but deformed, missing a good bite or two. I imagined it being hit by passing space objects, or perhaps Benji had a munch, thinking it was made out of cheese. As I squinted at it I could just make out a few smaller moons which were orbiting. Not only was life on Laridia different, but maybe their history of space-time was too.

As I sat there, my thoughts wandered like visions in the flickering flames of the fire. 'Why did you leave and what is keeping you both from returning to me?' I whimpered. I remembered my mother's gentle smile and my father's calming voice.

'Do you want some?' asked Benji, joining me to help keep watch, a portion of meat in one hand and a bit of fish in the other.

'No thanks, I'm not hungry,' I politely declined, eager to see the night's end and keep my internal battles at bay. 'Just thinking about.... things'

Benji nodded, sitting down beside me. 'Your parents?'

'Yeah,' I admitted, the weight of those words heavy on my heart. 'I just don't understand why they left.'

Mist was creeping in, rolling like a fog carpet towards us.

'Maybe they--'

'Quiet,' I whispered to Benji 'Don't move.'

The same horrifying clicking and flapping noises I had encountered before were all around us. In every direction. Patch was growling into the nothingness as screams, wails and yelps shattered my mind. More innocent victims had been claimed by the flying night stalkers moving in the direction of the mountain.

We all lay awake hoping to survive through to the morning.

Chapter Eighteen

At first light, our weary eyes gawked at our ever-changing surroundings. A vast array of all the colours under the rainbow sprouted out in all shapes and sizes from the floor below.

'How is this possible?' I said, nearly having to pinch myself.

'How lovely. The ideal conditions,' Spencer said, not in the faintest bit surprised by the bloom of toadstools and mushrooms.

'Shroomtastic,' Parker yelped, getting all excited.

'Toadally stool,' Jessie replied, even more excited than Parker.

'No eating, Benji. I know you'll eat anything,' said Frankie, firing a warning shot.

'But,' Benji was about to argue his case, but rubbed his tummy without thinking, then had to agree as the thought of yummy mushroom risotto made his mouth water. Do other kids dream of eating mushroom risotto?

'Seems we have our path,' I pointed over to some vegetation mirroring steps up to the higher levels, 'We can climb up and get across really quick if it can take our weight.'

We set off like supercharged lemmings skipping towards this bridge over the bog, forgetting all about the tribulations of the night before.

Clambering up to the top, the views were breathtaking. We could see the Zaamuk village chimneys piping away to the forest's edge and beyond.

Each stride caused a gravity-defying moon step as the soft, bouncy floor sprang us back up.

'Feels like a trampoline,' said Parker, who attempted a forward flip before landing flat on his back. He sprang straight to his feet. We all clapped.

The fungi forest was like a maze with overlapping stalks and platforms all entwined at different heights offering intricate turns and hidden rooms to be discovered as we made our way carefully across.

'Does anyone smell something?' I queried, as my nose started itching.

'Mushroom?' Spencer replied.

'No, something else.'

'I feel odd,' Benji said.

'You are odd,' Frankie joked.

'No, something's not quite right,' Parker said, before watching in horror as his sister's eyes started to glaze over. Then, giggling madly, she ran off, leaving them all behind.

'Where is she going?' Spencer asked, as Parker, Frankie and Benji wildly joined her, giggling uncontrollably like babies disappearing off around the next corner.

'What is happening to us?' I muttered as a sensation of childish glee began to course through my veins.

'Are you alright?' Spencer asked. His voice quivered.

I simply danced away singing, 'Can't catch me, I'm the mushroom man.' I left Spencer and Patch.

'Not alright then,' Spencer said, whilst noticing a haze of multi coloured spores releasing from our sky path. Spencer always suffered with allergies all year round and his concoction of anti-allergy medicines seemed to be keeping him rooted in reality.

Patch, even with his super sense of smell, seemed to be able to withstand the bright bacterium floating all around, as it only seemed to affect the humans in the group.

Spencer, too, seemed immune to the hallucinogenic particles released into the atmosphere; they were both okay as the cloud plumes became dense and choking.

'This is not good,' Spencer said, looking down at Patch, worried about his friends, 'I think we need to catch Boo first, then worry about the others.'

Patch set himself up like an Olympic sprinter and dashed off on the hunt. He was a hide-and-seek master, and it was not long before he had me pinned down, and I saw Spencer closing in. I had lost control of all sense of reality, repeating the same thing over and over.

'I'm a delicious truffle - please don't eat me.'

Spencer delved into my bag and grabbed the green goo pot, luckily, he never forgot anything with his eidetic memory.

'Green is for madness,' he repeated to himself trying to smear it across my face whilst I resisted.

'Don't be so sporing,' I was shouting, believing I was having the best time of my life and they were party poopers doing their best to spoil my mood. Seeping into my skin, I instantly vomited, flushing out the psychedelic poison inside me.

'You okay?' Spencer asked.

'Just about,' I said, scratching my throbbing head. 'Where are the others?'

Patch gave a little head shake and bounded off after the rest with Spencer and I in close pursuit.

Benji wasn't as quick as the others and when we found him, he was running in circles around the base of a giant toadstool.

'Are you stalking me?' he cried. Patch nipped at his heels.

'Benji stop struggling,' I persisted, as we took him down and gave him the medicine. After being sick, he shakily rose up, snapping out of his insane state of mind.

'I'm never gonna eat another mushroom as long as I live,' he said. Finally back to the same old Benji.

'Three more to go,' I sighed.

We found Jessie and Parker sitting quietly on the floor holding hands.

'I love you more than all the mushrooms in the world,' said Parker.

'I love you more than all the mushrooms in the universe,' Jessie whispered back. Then they gave each other a warm embrace.

'Must be a twin thing,' I said, as we quickly slapped the antidote across their brows.

Both of them hurled, before standing up sheepishly and pushing each other away in embarrassment.

'What happened?' both asked.

Frankie was next. She was sure to put up a fight and boy we were not disappointed.

The longer someone was exposed, the crazier they seemed to become. We had her backed into a corner and she was not going to go down easily, taking her axes from her belt and yelling at us.

'You will never take me. I thought you were fun-guys. I'll take you down,' she bellowed.

None of us would be taking her on in hand-to-hand combat, even when she wasn't possessed by rage demons, she would kick our butts.

'Patch, keep her there, I have an idea,' I instructed as he paced forward guarding her path, whilst everyone else stepped back to a safe distance.

'I'm sorry, Frankie,' I apologised, loading some soft mushroom debris into Jessie's flutedart, covering it in blue goo and asking her to give it a blowshot. We only had one chance at this, so here goes. Smash, splat, bang between the eyes, knocking her off her feet.

'Perfect aim, Jessie,' I applauded. Frankie was so enraged, she launched forward leaping over Patch straight at me.

She was about to land a knock-out blow, but she suddenly halted mid-swing. She dropped to her knees and soiled my trainers with stomach juices.

'Better them than you,' Parker said with a smile as Frankie's red mist dissipated and she returned to normal.

'Blimey, remind me never to make you upset,' Benji whispered, still cowering from the episode.

We could feel the sun beating down upon us with a punishing heat. The once sturdy walkway was drying out, no longer bouncy, but brittle and now crumbling beneath our feet with every step.

'Something's wrong,' I shouted out as the pathway already trodden seemed to be disintegrating like a collapsing bridge encroaching rapidly behind us, 'Run!' I yelled, as our once solid footpath across the plains was rumbling and crashing down all around us. We all made a desperate dash for sanctuary.

The team were now hot-footing it to freedom, hurdling gaping holes that appeared in the ground. Ducking beneath falling stems that had once supported the walkway, now slicing through it like a knife through warm butter.

Hearts pounding, it was a do-or-die version of school sports day as adrenaline kicked in. We all managed to cross the finish line for a photo finish just before the whole fungi forest fell to dust, crashing to the floor.

'We were close to toast,' said Parker, panting from pure exhaustion.

'You think?' Frankie retorted, trying to catch her breath.

'Everyone accounted for?' I said, as I quickly counted heads.

Benji and Jessie were lying down exhausted like they had completed a marathon. Patch was darting around between us with nervous excitement, looking ahead as the foot of the mountain now lay at our door.

'This is it,' I cried. 'Now, one way or another we will find our answers.'

Chapter Nineteen

The sky stretched endlessly above us, an unbroken expanse of blistering blue, with not a single cloud to offer relief. The sun bore down mercilessly, its scorching rays pressing against our skin like a relentless weight. Every breath felt thick and dry, the air shimmering with heat waves that wavered across the horizon, making the distant landscape dance like a mirage. We needed to rest, but there was no escaping the punishing heat wrapping around us.

As we huddled to discuss our next move, I recalled how my parents would solve problems together. Their teamwork was impeccable. I hoped I could lead my friends with the same wisdom.

'We should set up camp,' I announced to the group, hoping a little rest would lighten the mood and keep spirits up.

'Yeah, I'm more than happy to delay dying a little longer,' Frankie said, collapsing to the floor.

Whilst resting, I looked at the mountain ahead. From a distance, the sun's rays had made it glow pink and inviting, but there was also a distinct, desolate, barren feeling of greyness, keeping away unwanted guests.

It gave me an eerie, nervous feeling. Compared to the rest of the landscape on Laridia, it looked out of place, simply put here by some higher power. It looked deserted.

'Patch, are we in the right place?' I asked the little fellow, 'There doesn't seem to be anything here.' He stood up defiantly barking at the colossal rock formation ahead.

'Okay, don't need to tell me twice,' I accepted that as a yes, and I started getting ready to move out.

'Frankie, are you okay to scout ahead with me to see what we are up against?'

'Count me in,' she replied.

'Be careful,' came the wise words from Spencer.

Benji gave a clear instruction, 'Make sure you come back to get us and don't try anything too heroic my dear hero boy.'

Everyone had found a shady spot to hide from the relentless scorching sun, which burned down, turning the ground into a sweltering furnace.

Jessie and Parker nodded in agreement, their eyes hopeful and their faces sweaty, looking at us both.

Towards the lions' den, the three of us headed.

Drawing closer, we were a short throw from the base of the mountain. Greeting us was a wall of translucent white, curving its way around the bottom and rising high into the sky. It formed a protective dome around the mysterious mound like some sort of force field, preventing us from coming closer.

'Don't like the look of this, maybe we need to find a way of disabling it, so we can get through,' I whispered to Frankie.

Before I had even finished my sentence, she swung at it impatiently with her axe looking to carve us a way past. Instead, there was no resistance and she fell through, disappearing completely from sight with Patch leaping through after her.

I edged through the light to join my team. Frankie and Patch were waiting, looking back in amazement. The wall had simply been a holographic projection of a mountain image to fool and ward off anyone from entering. Through the illusion it became clear we had uncovered its true identity.

Towering all around us was a futuristic base of operations. Sleek, advanced metal curved structures like pods glinted in the sunlight.

The only indication of activity came from glowing vents protruding from the surface, releasing gas, hissing and churning like a mammoth manufacturing machine.

Chapter Twenty

What was it cooking?

A sharp tang of heated metal filled the air, mingling with the acrid scent of burning fuel. Hissing jets of steam escaped from hidden vents, their rhythmic exhalations echoing through the towering metal landscape ahead. A sprawling metropolis of gleaming steel stretched before us, its polished surfaces reflecting the harsh sunlight in blinding streaks. The air shimmered with heatwaves, distorting the intricate web of pipes, platforms, and towering structures that pulsed with an eerie mechanical life.

The air temperature felt like an oven, and beads of sweat formed across our brows. It was obviously not native to the primitive nature of Laridia and it had been put here for a purpose and our job was to find out why.

'Look, Boo, your bracelet is glowing,' Frankie said. As I looked down, there was only one word shining through, 'Darkfall'. It sent shudders through my body, though it quickly faded.

'What did it say?' Frankie enquired.

'I'm not even sure, but something to do with the dark I was warned about, so we need to keep our wits about us. Let's go for a closer look,' I instructed, creeping forward with Patch glued to my side ready for anything.

There was no vegetation around, red sandy floors as if the earth had been scorched to cinders and various rock formations dotted around with large, still, beastly statues on them overlooking our path.

'They look real,' whispered Frankie, looking at the bat-like, gargoyle, winged beasts, 'They look really real,' she repeated, as she drew nearer to one, 'They sound really real too,' she grimaced as heavy breathing could be heard from the beasts sitting dormant.

'Quiet,' I whispered back.

Tiptoeing on through, we reached the outer edge of the structure. Placing my hands on the shell, I could feel the whirring ripples as vibrations from inside shook the walls.

What on earth was going on inside this structure and how were we going to get in? There were no visible doorways. This was no normal building.

'There must be a way in,' I said, challenging us to find it. All of a sudden, alarm bells went off. 'What did you touch?' I said, glaring at Frankie.

'Wasn't me,' she said, jumping back. We both took cover out of sight. Patch had taken refuge across the way from us.

A once plain, solid wall ahead began lifting up from the ground like an aircraft hangar and we braced ourselves. Out of the doorway came a slim humanlike figure with a dark aura, mist emanating from its trail as it stepped out into the open.

A non-distinct robed and hooded humanoid character with normal facial features was looking up at the gargoyle guards, but when it raised its hands, their eyes began to glow a fiendish green.

The demonic beasts rose. Heads first. Their eyes were glowing emerald green, as if they were being communicated with telepathically.

The alarms had not woken them up, but somehow this conjurer was able to control them remotely. Within moments, they had awakened and taken flight away from their perches.

We watched, staying hidden. Out of the corner of my eye I spotted Patch sneaking past the unaware darkling into the void beyond.

The dark figure then lowered its arms and turned around. It went back to the lair with the door lowering behind it, preventing us from getting through and trapping Patch inside.

'What on earth?' said Frankie, throwing her arms up in the air, 'I thought you said they were night stalkers, it's not even nighttime.'

'It looks like the dark being had sent them out to hunt something or someone,' I said, knowing full well our team could be in danger, 'Just hope our friends will be okay, but we can't risk going back now. We've come too far and need to push on.'

The question now was how. Rattling noises could be heard in the pod wall overhead and a second later one of the lower vents popped out crashing to the floor between us.

A friendly face appeared gazing down at us, sounding off with a quiet gruff. Our little mascot had found a way into the fortress. Giving Frankie a quick boost up, she reached down and helped me up. I squeezed into the hole in the wall.

We were in. The vent was a tight, pitch-black crawling space. We were blind following our hairy guide into the abyss.

Weaving up and down with some tight, awkward bends, we finally saw light as we approached a grate looking down into a dingy room below. Giving it a hefty boot, I managed to kick it down to the floor below and we carefully lowered our way down.

The room was lit by some glowing cubes piled up in a corner to one side, each one about the size of a basketball. I could taste metal in the air as the charred scent of scorched steel was intoxicating. Looking closely, you could see energy rushing around inside, trapped and waiting to be freed.

Frankie picked one up, 'Very light, like there is helium inside, Boo,' she said, throwing it up into the air, then giving it a stern shake, which sent surges of light coursing around inside, bouncing off the sides like a spirit trying to escape.

'Like some sort of weird battery or energy storage,' I concluded, 'Best not to drop one, who knows what's inside,' I warned her. She carefully placed it back down.

We were in a small storage room with an open doorway on one side. There were dozens of workers in an extra-long corridor running back and forth with trolleys, some full of glowing cubes and some empty.

'Don't let them see you,' Frankie warned, but it was already too late. One was coming right for us! No escape now as it hurtled into the room with a full trolley.

We were standing in the middle of the room as it entered. Stranded with nowhere to hide. There was nothing we could do. The worker rushed right up to our feet before halting abruptly as if someone pressed a pause button.

A weird AI drone robot with a single wheel beneath it for propulsion was balancing in front of us. The bot had a thin, cylindrical body split into four revolving mid-sections. Each revolving plate was sporting a set of dangly pincer-shaped grabbers, making it look like an eight-limbed metal octopus.

The worker bot did not seem to care who or what we were. Waiting for us to move out of its way. It gave off annoyed warning beeps, so we took a step to the side. Thankfully, it continued on its merry way, pushing its trolley up to the stack.

Standing between the trolley and the stack, it grabbed a cube in each set of arms. The body spun, placing them neatly before spinning back and forth until the trolley was empty. Then off it trundled to its next assigned task.

Stepping out into the corridor, we were dodging incoming traffic from all directions as the bots frantically rushed between jobs. The corridor was so long that the end could not be seen by the human eye and there were open doorways filled with these curious cubes. Were we in a giant storage facility? None of it made sense.

'So, which way now, oh fearless leader?' Frankie asked, raising her voice over the racket of trolley carts grinding along the tough metallic floor.

I was about to point out that the empty ones were going in one direction and ask if we should follow. Patch was already one step ahead, hitching a ride on the back of a bot and rolling off into the distance.

'Why not?' Frankie said, pouncing on the next passer-by and hanging on to the various appendages, setting off in hot pursuit. 'Giddy up,' she yelped.

'Wait for me,' I blurted out, as I perched myself on the next trolley dolly. And away we went down a labyrinth of corridors, rooms and worker machines. Round and round we went like a conveyor belt between the various aisles, bypassing one another over and over as we went up and down levels.

My metal steed was finally slowing down. A few hairpin turns later the hallway opened up into a massive open space. Doorways all around, teeming with these bots popping in and out like a colony of ants harvesting for their master.

In the centre of the hive, we found the Queen. A goliath glowing spherical machine suspended in the air. Hundreds of tube-like tentacles delivering completed cubes to the floor to be collected by the drones. It was like something straight out of a science fiction movie.

Patch, Frankie and I could see up ahead, so we gracefully exited our vehicles - only just in time. Out of reach of the mechanical octopus.

'Mystery mountain must be a manufacturing plant,' I said.

'For what though?' Frankie questioned me, as we all took a second to survey our surroundings.

Chapter Twenty-One

Towards the top of the sphere, there was an open platform overlooking the entire plant.

'That is where we need to get to. Maybe it's a control room of some sort?' I pointed out.

'Yeah, but who's controlling all of this, Boo?' Frankie asked. She ran her hand through her hair and her brow furrowed.

'Patch, can you find us a way up there?' I asked and Patch replied with a confident head bob, and off he set.

Not long after, he returned with an alternative route, bypassing the motorway mayhem of the busy worker bees through a hallway on the other side. When entering I noticed strange symbols above the doorway.

'What do you think it says, Boo?' Frankie asked.

'Says no dogs allowed, sorry Patch,' I joked.

'Really?'

'Of course not, but it probably means we are going in the right direction,' I said, as I hoped for stairs or even better a lift. Reaching the end of the hallway, a spiral walkway like a helter-skelter greeted us, winding its way up to the level above.

Round and round, up and up we circled until we reached the next level. Entering another large open room filled with coffin-shaped containers packed neatly in tight rows, covering the entire floor area.

It was hard to make out too much with limited light as we squeezed by, but a feeling of dread was flowing through our fingers looking at these lifeless casings.

Whatever life may have been in them now looked to be long extinguished and we didn't fancy waking the dead, so we pressed on through another doorway on the opposite side leading to another open area.

The next space, larger than the first, was housing hundreds of caskets. The whole room was lit with an amber radiance emitting from each of them. Approaching I noticed they each had a glass panel front and what lay inside shocked me to the core. Floating in a clear gel liquid were unconscious tribe people connected to a monitoring station via various tubes and wires with blood flowing out and back through again, as if their life essence was being harvested.

'They are harvesting people,' I announced, rushing around checking each case and sure enough every one of them was occupied.

'Yuck,' said Frankie, doing her best to avoid looking.

Patch had jumped up barking at them doing his best to awaken the sleeping science experiments, but to no avail.

The tribespeople entrapped were from lots of different groups and had diverse body features to the ones we had already met on our travels. Some had giant claws instead of hands, a few had larger heads with even bigger teeth and one even had an extra set of arms, but nonetheless it seemed they all possessed something which was worth reaping.

'We need to find a way to save them all,' I said, vowing to myself we would prevail, but pessimism soon set in as we passed through room after room, each one full to the brim with these horrors.

The rooms were all curving around the outside wall adjacent to the queen hall and the reservoirs seemed to source the golden amber needed to power the cuboids.

We hoped to find the control room and put an end to this madness.

'Looks like they aren't finished,' said Frankie, pointing to lots of unlit enclosures yet to be filled and then turning to see a few human-shaped figures standing over some of the lit units.

'Get away from them,' I screamed as I rushed at the figures.

They were medical androids with four arms instead of two each with a specific tool for slicing and dicing, poking and prodding at the victims, getting them ready to harvest. I barged into one sending it crashing to the floor in a heap. Parts sprayed across the deck.

Red lights flashed on the remaining droids as they had been alerted to danger, and the last two started converging on me, blades and drills spinning wildly.

'You should not be out of your chamber,' came a robot voice, 'Return at once or be eliminated.'

Patch, now a flying Ninja, had scooped up an arm from the fallen bot and launched himself through the air. Striking one clean across the nose with a big, literal 'slap in the face', taking its head clean off. It then walked around like a headless chicken before keeling over.

'Good boy,' I shouted, 'You showed that robot who's boss.'

The other was still coming for me. Taking a step back I stumbled to the floor as it approached. I shuffled backwards against the wall, kicking frantically to knock it off balance.

I was about to be put to the meat grinder as the razor-sharp tools edged towards my face.

'Frankieeee, Paaatch, help!'

Frankie's axes split straight through the robot's head, lodging it into the wall behind.

'And that is how it's done ladies and gentlemen,' Frankie said, taking a bow.

'Thought I was going to be chop-booey for a moment there,' I said.

'English-speaking torture robots, whatever next?' Frankie chuckled.

Patch was now yapping for attention standing aloft one of the caskets which was now oozing gel through a small crack in the side. We'd interrupted the process and the person inside was thrashing about panicking like a fish out of water.

'Hold on, we'll save you,' I voiced through the glass, 'Frankie, hand me your axe,' and as she passed to me, I used the spiked end to jam between the panels to lever it open. Gushing gel liquid splashed over the floor around us as it drained from the chamber.

The jelly-covered figure sat bolt upright, gasping for air. I recognised that face. Was it really? Yes, it was!

'Lu-Ni, it's me,' I said, as I wiped his eyes clear.

Once he was back with us, without missing a beat, he smartly replied, 'I always knew you were the one,' he spluttered out, dragging me in for a manly embrace, 'and who's your girlfriend?'

'She's not my girlfriend,' I snapped, feeling my face redden, 'I mean, she's a girl, and she is my friend,' before getting completely tongue-tied. She stepped in.

'I'm Frankie, one of Boo's friends, we all foolishly followed him into his portal thingy, got a bit lost, but somehow found each other. The long and short of it is, we are here to rescue you'.

'Where are we?' Lu-Ni queried, still in a bit of a daze.

'Well, you know the mysterious mountain? Well, it was not even a real mountain. It was a front for a tribe juicing farm.' I explained.

Looking around he could see what I meant with the minefield of juicing chambers, but I continued to explain in brief our journey to get here and what we had encountered.

'So, the Darkness had found Laridia?' asked Lu-Ni as he hung his head.

I tried to stay positive, 'We don't know what they are doing here or why they took you, but we will stop them together. I promise.'

All the other units were completely sealed despite our best efforts to pry another one open.

'We need to find the master controls to get them released,' I said with confidence, as we made our way to the next staircase to see what the next floor from hell would provide.

We saw a bucket conveyor humming and clanking along.

'Looks like they are being sent somewhere above us,' I noted.

'What gave it away, Meatball?' Frankie said, being clever.

'So they are draining us dry and putting us into little boxes? Who does this?' said Lu-Ni with a shocked look on his face.

'Just like milking cows I guess,' Frankie said.

Continuing, we darted through a few remaining rooms on this level stuffed full of empty cubes, robot parts and some powered down backup droids. Commotion and humdrum could be heard coming from ahead.

'Can you hear the noise?' I asked as we sneakily entered the final room to gauge what was making such a racket.

Lo and behold, it was a large holding cell with electric field bars blocking anything in and out, plus two humanoid guard units marching back and forth protecting the precious cargo. What was so important inside it would need two guards, while the rest of the facility we were free to roam?

We managed to tuck neatly out of sight behind a wall of piled up scrap bots. Peering over I checked out the enemy lines for weakness.

'Armed guards,' Lu-Ni answered, clenching his fist angrily until his knuckles cracked so loudly that both guards snapped to attention. They looked in our general direction. We crouched down.

Loud steps could be heard as they drew closer and pulsating neon blue lasers were scanning the room around us as we stayed hidden.

'How are we going to get past them?' Frankie whispered.

Patch wasn't hanging about waiting for them to catch us and strolled out calmly, plodding into full view. They locked onto him like a hawk and assessed the danger before zeroing in on him. Their new target.

They took aim, unleashing a sonic boom as a pulse of electromagnetic force exploded towards him. Patch was too quick as they began pummelling power strikes around the room. Debris was flying everywhere, and the boxes we were taking refuge behind were shattered. We were now out in the open with nothing to protect us. Sitting ducks.

Fortunately, Patch had them distracted as they hit everything. The nimble pooch leapt like a leprechaun, delicately dodging each wave of attack.

I picked up a few heavy nuts and bolts scattered across the ground, loaded them into my slingshot, and swung with speed and precision. As I was doing this, Lu-Ni had launched himself into the air, arms out, gliding high above our heads like a flying squirrel towards his target.

At the same time, we both landed the fatal blows. My projectile penetrated the armour plating, ripping through the chest of one. Lu-Ni grabbed the other by its head, lifting it clean off the ground. He smashed it against the roof above and executed a perfect landing any gymnast would be proud of.

A chorus of clapping and cheering could be heard from inside the cell, and, looking through the force field, we could make out four childlike shapes bouncing up and down at the grand spectacle of the battle they had witnessed.

Great for an emotional reunion!

'Fancy meeting you guys here,' came the distinct comical voice of Benji.

Jessie uncontrollably yelled like a mega fan excitedly, 'Boo, you beautiful beast I knew you'd rescue us.'

'Again,' Parker added, twisting his brace.

'How did you guys end up here?' I asked, although I sort of already knew the answer, and I was right. A story of the winged, misty monsters attacking the camp followed.

'We were then dropped out of the air by these winged brutes into a skyroom and robot guards escorted us here, locking us up,' Benji explained. He took off his cracked glasses and frowned.

'What else did you see up there?' I asked, for more information.

Three ashamed faces stared back at me, their memories blurred by shock. Yet, as always, good old Mr Reliable Spencer stepped forward into view.

'We were dropped on the top floor. There were two dark-robbed men talking to one another over by a bright white orb in a stand. It looked like it powered the control system over by the viewing gallery and there were two human-like robot guards that rounded us up.' Spencer paused for a moment to access his memory bank before he continued.

'Odd-looking colourful boxes kept being delivered. Each time another robot picked them up and pushed them through a shadowy oval doorway. They disappeared. One of the black robes pointed at us, muttering something, and then walked through the doorway and vanished too,' said Spencer, finishing his account without taking a breath.

'Vanished? Do you mean through a portal?' I questioned, as my eyes lit up. Could there be others wielding magic doorways to other places too?

'Yeah, sure maybe, it was larger than ours, and unlike ours, it stayed open. Oh yeah and smelled like ammonia if that helps.'

'Ammonia?' I said, confused.

'He means wee,' Jessie said, saving us time as Parker looked a little red-faced.

'I was proper scared,' Parker admitted and who could blame him.

'Glad someone was paying attention,' I responded, and I was happy Spencer could give me some much-needed reconnaissance of what we were going to face above.

Chapter Twenty-Two

First, we needed to free our fellow adventurers.

'Everyone, this is Lu-Ni, and Lu-Ni, this is everyone,' I said, gesturing a greeting between our two clans. 'Now let's see about getting you all out of here.' I looked around for a switch or button, but found none.

No one had really noticed Patch, who was parading around us all through the force field and back out again without a care in the world. It was clear he was immune to its deathly beams.

Lu-Ni was the first to spot him. He bravely grabbed hold of the bars, receiving an almighty zap. His hands were grilled like a shibok-kebab and the smell of burnt flesh engulfed the room.

Releasing his grip, he was blown back across the room. Lightning bolts exited his body.

'I can see where he gets his loony name from,' Parker laughed. We watched Lu-Ni get up shocked but unscathed and I was glad he was still in one piece.

'If he can't break those bars, then what can we do?' asked Jessie as worry spread across her face.

Benji brightly stepped forward. He knew he had an idea, 'Can't we use those weapons?'

Frankie walked over and wrestled one out of the droid's grip.

'Stand back everyone,' she yelled. Everyone curled up in the corner of the cell, fearful of what could happen. Jessie used poor Spencer as a shield.

'I'm not sure that's a good idea,' Spencer spoke out, but he was too late. Frankie had let rip and a thunderclap reverberated out of the cosmic cannon, blasting her off her feet, frazzling her hair and throwing her straight back into my open arms.

All the lights flickered in the room, and a powering-down sound came as it had punched a hole right through. We were finally free.

Parker stepped out, 'Aww, look at you two lovebirds,' as I quickly propped Frankie back onto her feet.

Jessie looked at her, 'Thanks Franks, I like what you've done with your hair.' We all stared at her hair. It was as if the backdraft had forced static through it and fluffed it in a fan like a peacock.

Benji couldn't resist boasting, 'Genius! Genius is my middle name.'

'No, it's not your middle name,' came back Spencer, 'Your middle name is Kelsey, Benji Kelsey Archer.'

'A girl's name, that would explain a few things,' Parker said with a chuckle.

'It's not a girl's name, it's a unisex name,' Jessie said, defending him.

Benji had to admit, 'Well, it was after my Gran, who passed away before I was born.' Everyone went quiet.

We were a full team again, a force to be reckoned with.

'The super six are now the superb seven,' Parker said, now upbeat about our chances, but he got an angry bark off Patch as if he was dismayed at not being counted in. 'Okay, okay, sorry, the sensational seven and a half,' Parker said, giving Patch a pat on the head.

'Okay, we know what we are up against, and we need to make a plan,' I voiced to the group as we all fell to our knees to discuss what move to make next.

'We run in guns a-blazin,' Frankie suggested, desiring the full army frontal attack.

'Okay calm down Frankie. Whatever it is up there already knows we are here, as we've hardly been quiet,' I said, as I tried to curb her enthusiasm.

'We should split into teams,' I said, thinking it would be a good idea to divide us all. There was no point in our getting caught at the same time.

'Shotgun the big grey fellow,' Benji said, as he squeezed the bulging muscles on Lu-Ni's arm.

'You can't shotgun a person,' Jessie scolded, 'anyway, I'll take Frankie, we girls need to stick together.'

'Spencer, Parker, which team do you want to go with? Patch and I will be on the other team' I said, giving them a choice.

'Can't leave my sister, I'll get grounded if I don't bring her back in one piece,' Parker said, grabbing his sister's arm. So the teams were sorted. Now we needed a plan.

'I suggest one team goes to the front and causes a distraction, whilst the rest of us hitch a ride up with the lift system, so we can come at it from two sides,' I said boldly.

Everyone seemed to agree with my idea.

Chapter Twenty-Three

'Frankie, axes. Twins, cannons. Blast anything hostile. Spencer, go up and wave your stick around,' I said, knowing full well Spencer couldn't intimidate a mouse but needed a job.

'Lu-Ni, Patch, Benji, and I will sneak up and try to subdue it. Maybe we can learn something.'

'Where's Spencer?' I scanned the room. 'Was no one watching Spencer?' I had forgotten he took things literally. 'Go, go, go!'

The rest of Spencer's team grabbed their weapons and bolted after him. My squad jumped into the elevator and executed the pincer movement. Grinding gears and crunching cogs echoed around us, so much for stealth!

As I surfaced, Spencer stood waving his stick—more mental than menacing. Somehow, it worked. The robed figure was focused on him, but enemy reinforcements had arrived. Three towering sentinels, bristling with weaponry, aimed at our poor, oblivious Spencer.

Meanwhile, a worker bot yanked me into the room, mistaking me for cargo. Then, Patch landed on top of me, tail wagging. Benji, hanging upside down, swung toward us next. Lu-Ni, without hesitation, tore off the bot's limbs and kicked it aside.

'Got you, little human,' Lu-Ni said, freeing Benji from a robot arm and setting him down gently.

The robed figure noticed us and ordered his guards to fire. Before I could yell 'run,' Frankie burst through, tackling Spencer out of the line of fire. The twins stormed in, unleashing beams of shockwaves. Chaos erupted.

We were outmatched. Blind firing from cover, dodging artillery, scrambling for a plan. Lu-Ni hurled droid parts like a catapult while Benji reloaded more scrap for ammo.

'Wonder what these glowing things do,' Benji mused, shoving an energy cube into Lu-Ni's grip.

'Beeeeenjiiii noooooo!' I cried out.

Too late. The cube crashed, cracked, and imploded, sucking in everything around it, before erupting in a silent shockwave. The blast threw us all to the ground. My ears rang. Smoke filled the room. The walls were on fire.

I staggered up. Two of the three sentinels were down. The last loomed over us, weapons locked. Then, salvation came in the form of Patch. The little critter dragged a live wire, sizzling at the end. He darted under the bot and fried it from the inside out. Benji poked it. It toppled over.

'Not so tough now, huh?' Benji taunted. It twitched on the floor. He dove behind Lu-Ni.

We regrouped, battle-worn but standing. Our adversary, a single-robed figure, hadn't even flinched.

'Everyone okay?' I asked.

'Peachy,' Frankie said, axes crossed.

'Alive,' the twins echoed, blasters ready.

'Getting there,' Benji grinned, brandishing utensils like he was about to carve a turkey.

'Time to free my people,' Lu-Ni declared.

'Ermm, not really okay,' Spencer coughed, covered in ash. 'I got shot at and almost exploded. My favourite shirt is ruined. Also, I lost my stick. Just go on without me.'

Patch retrieved it, wagging his tail.

'Oh great, my club,' Spencer muttered.

'Now it's a firestick,' Parker noted, pointing at the aflame ends.

I stepped forward. 'Time to end this. Let's stop this Lord of Darkness before he hurts anyone else.'

Frankie yelled, 'Come on, Dark Lord, give us your best shot!'

Jessie whispered, 'Please, Dark Lord, be gentle.'

The robed figure removed his hood. A pale, hairless man. No panic in his eyes. Just cold calculation.

'That's it? A bald old man?' Parker scoffed, smirking to himself.

'Don't judge a book by its cover,' Spencer warned. 'Might be a dark wizard.'

Frankie hurled an axe. The man raised his arms. Tattoos burned into his wrists—twin solar eclipses. His eyes flared green. A plasma shield flickered into existence. The axe slowed, hovered, then shot back at us, nearly skewering Benji.

The twins fired. Their blasts fizzled into nothing. Lu-Ni charged, but his attacks moved as if through water. The robed figure effortlessly clotheslined him and drop-kicked him across the room.

'Weak mortals,' he boomed, voice shaking the ground. 'You will perish.'

He lifted a hand. We were yanked into the air, limbs frozen. A crushing force squeezed the breath from our lungs. My friends' faces contorted in fear. My vision blurred. This was it.

Then, a growl. Low. Deep. Rising into a hurricane. Patch. His tiny body unleashed a storm of sonic shockwaves, shattering the dark force holding us captive. We collapsed, gasping.

Patch advanced, his scream pushing the robed figure back. The villain's shield cracked.

'It cannot be,' he hissed. 'You were destroyed.'

Desperate, he siphoned energy from the orb, recharging himself. A blast sent Patch flying, and he lay motionless.

'Oh no!' I rushed to him. Patch, our secret weapon, was down.

The villain laughed, gloating. 'You will never stop the darkness. We will drain your worlds dry. Oblivion is near.'

My wrist buzzed. A single word: Light. It appeared and a chill ran down my spine.

The hope hoop on my wrist flared, connecting me to the orb. A surge of energy rushed through me. My body glowed. I spun my sling, light gathering with every revolution.

'He looks possessed,' Benji muttered.

'Like an angel,' Parker and Jessie whispered.

Lu-Ni nodded. 'The Angel of Hope.'

'Just kick his ass, Boo,' Frankie said.

I released my shot. A fireball erupted, obliterating the dark shield, burning through his robes. He screamed, breaking from the orb's grasp. His eyes dimmed.

In a final act of cowardice, he unleashed a smokescreen and fled to a portal. I caught a glimpse beyond—a war-torn city, storm clouds, stockpiles of stolen energy cubes. Something terrible was coming.

As the portal began to close, the orb rose from its stand and drifted towards it, as though being summoned back

'I'll take that,' Spencer said, snagging it midair. Then, with perfect comedic timing, he jabbed his burning stick into the breach. 'You can have this though. Goodbye.' The portal was sealed with a fizzle.

For now.

Chapter Twenty-Four

The orb was now missing from its stand, and the whole facility began to shake! Machines groaned and sputtered, their lights flickering like frightened fireflies. Without the orb's endless energy, everything was slowing down... stopping.

We dashed to the edge of the platform, hearts racing, just in time to see the enormous sphere tipping over. It wobbled for a moment, then CRASH! It hit the ground with a thunderous boom! Its long, twisting limbs fell limp, smashing against the floor like giant stone pillars, sending tremors through the entire building. The walls shuddered, the floor rumbled beneath our feet, and it felt like the whole place was about to crumble!

'It's coming down!' I shouted as the roof above us groaned and split, jagged cracks racing across the ceiling. 'Everyone out, NOW!'

Lu-Ni didn't hesitate. He dropped to his knees beside Patch, who was still motionless on the cold floor. 'Come on, buddy,' he murmured, gently brushing the dust from Patch's face. 'I've got you.' With tender care, he scooped Patch into his arms, cradling him. My heart melted.

'He's so light,' Lu-Ni muttered, tightening his grip as the walls trembled. Patch's head lolled against his shoulder, his breathing shallow but steady.

'Let's make tracks!' Frankie shouted, and we all bolted for the exit. The whole facility was collapsing around us—steel beams groaning, sparks flying, the floor buckling beneath our feet.

'My people,' Lu-Ni announced, holding Patch close as we raced against time, desperate not to be buried under the falling wreckage. 'We cannot leave them.'

'We will try and save everyone,' I assured him.

Entering the crypts area, we saw that all the chambers without power had opened, releasing an army of dazed and confused tribespeople.

'Wow, it's people-ly,' Benji said. We looked at the giant flash mob all released from their slumber.

'People-ly is not even a real word,' Spencer snapped, whilst ushering the zombies towards the exits.

Lu-Ni was shouting instructions at his stricken brothers as they all lined up to follow like sheep heading for freedom.

'It seems to be working,' I said.

Jessie and Parker led the way with the horde hot on their heels, like a fire drill, making sure no one was left behind.

Spencer, Lu-Ni and I were at the back making sure everyone got out ahead of us.

The roof started falling in around us. In the chaos, Lu-Ni, Spencer and I got split from the rest of the party. The cave-in had blocked our path. We had no way to pass through despite Lu-Ni trying his best to heave slabs of rubble out of the way.

'We need to go back and see if there is another exit,' I conceded, turning around so we hotfooted it back to the control room. The whole building was on the verge of collapse.

After reaching the control room platform, we peered over the railings. In the main hall we could make out the mass congregation of people fleeing towards the exit.

They called out our names. They were trapped and did not know our whereabouts or where to go next.

'We are up here,' Spencer bellowed down to the team. The shouting had now awoken Patch from the knockout blow, a little shaken but no permanent damage done as he bounced back into my arms to give me a loving lick.

'You saved us little buddy,' I whispered in his ear, 'but we are not home and dry yet.'

I looked around desperate to find a way to escape. A few overhanging tubes and cables were dangling from the ceiling, inviting us to use them as a Tarzan-style rope swing.

'We can swing over to the top of the ball and slide down,' I said optimistically, 'I'll go first with Patch, and you follow my lead.'

With Patch slung over my shoulders like a pelt, I took a few steps back. Then I lurched forward, launching myself into the wide-open space. I grabbed hold of the make-do vines. After a few swings, I crossed the cables, shimmied onto the top of the sphere, and slid down to safety

'Come on, it's your turn Spencer,' I beckoned.

'I am not doing it, sorry,' was his defiant reply.

'Come on Spencer, you can do it,' I pleaded.

'I mean I can't do it. I was rubbish in gym. My only muscles are my intellect,' he insisted.

Lu-Ni butted in, 'You are coming with me then.' He picked up Spencer, not waiting for permission, and leapt like a skydiver straight from the balcony with his unwilling passenger clinging piggyback for dear life.

We thought we had heard some weird sounds on this adventure, but nothing could have prepared us for the ear-shattering screams from Spencer as they fell in free-fall.

Lu-Ni, half smiling, left it to the last minute to open his glide-wings and perform a professional parachute landing into the swarm of spectators.

Spencer scuttled down. Then stood. He watched me sphere-sliding to meet him at the bottom. We were all together again.

'Afraid of heights hey Spence?' Benji said.

'I enjoy heights actually, it's the falling from great heights I am not particularly fond of,' he responded.

'Got me beat in hitting those high notes, Spencer,' Jessie joined in, as she imitated his screams.

'Ignore them, I think you were brave,' Parker said, patting him on the shoulder.

Lu-Ni and I looked at each other shaking our heads.

'You sounded like a howling wolf being strangled through a megaphone,' Frankie berated him.

The gathering in the main hall was now a deathtrap as chunks of the ceiling came crashing down around us, smashing into the ground and causing panic in the horde. I thought I saw my dad. My real Dad in the crowd! I rubbed my eyes, in total shock. When I opened my eyes again – he was gone. I was losing it. We needed an exit and fast.

'Escaping through the vent might be good. I'm worried about the numbers though. We might not make it before this place collapses,' I suggested, but was open to other ideas.

Patch, now back with us, darted up to Benji, who was leaning against the wall, having a quick meat snack to calm his nerves. He jumped up on his leg and barked at him.

'Bark... bark... bark,' Benji played back, 'Yes you can have some,' he said, throwing a morsel on the floor. 'Good boy,' he continued. Patch ignored the food and kept barking. 'I think your dog may be broken.'

'Benji, I think he wants you to move,' I yelled. Benji shifted away and looked back, embarrassed. He had been leaning on the control panel for the hangar doors the whole time!

'Good find Benji,' I mocked, pushing the button and hey presto. Nothing.

'No power,' Spencer snapped, pointing out the obvious.

Looking around, everything had ground to a halt, and the once busy machines were standing as lifeless as statues.

'I have an idea,' Frankie said, running up to one of the trolleys and grabbing a few glowing cubes. She then placed them neatly against the doorway of departure, 'I think this should be enough.'

We gathered everyone to the opposite side of the hall for safety.

'Who would like to do the honours?' I queried as we kept one back ready to use as a hand grenade.

Again, I thought I saw my dad. I shook my head. Was I losing my mind?

Benji said, 'My vote is on the big scary looking fella,' as Scarface, now free from captivity, came into view, towering head and shoulders above most others, pushing his way past. The big brute of a specimen was storming towards me, looking as happy as ever before, suddenly taking a knee, bowing his head and muttering some words out loud.

'He praises you and your companions for saving them,' Lu-Ni translated.

The room fell silent as all the tribesmen took a knee in homage.

'Can you tell him it's not over yet. They can thank us later and I'd like to borrow his throwing arm for a minute,' I said, as I pointed towards the pile and placed the explosive box in his iron grip. Scarface stood to his feet pleased to help. Like an Olympic shot putter, he launched it with pinpoint precision. It was as if he threw things for a living.

'Bombs away,' I shouted, as it connected with the other blocks. We expected the fireworks show of the century.

'Well, is something going to happen?' cried Parker, walking forward.

'Wait for it, bro,' Jessie said, pulling him back.

Crackles could be heard slicing through the air like a burning fuse ready to ignite as we watched in anticipation. They lit up like ferocious firecracker dominoes, one after another, tearing down the whole wall. As the wall crumbled, it revealed views of the Laridia beyond and the smell of freedom.

'You were only supposed to blow the doors off,' I laughed as we all stormed out into the open air. The heat was still unbearable as the sun's rays continued to bake us like biscuits.

Looking back, we had made it out in the nick of time. The once mysterious mountain collapsed in on itself, demolishing the taint of the dark from this land.

'Just how many of those blocky thingies were in there?' Benji asked. Everyone turned with bated breath.

'A lot,' answered Frankie, as the ground trembled. It ripped open like fault lines on the earth's crust. The once mountainous landscape sank into the ground, and a force like an atom bomb ravaged the lands around us. A plume of hot winds, scorching the terrain headed our way. A giant sinkhole was forming, spreading out in all directions from the epicentre. It dragged all life into a web of destruction.

'That cannot be anything good,' I said, turning to bolt in the opposite direction.

Fleeing in terror, hundreds of little legs worked overtime, not to be plunged into the pit of doom.

Everyone scrambled as far away as they could, but some stragglers were not so fortunate. The ground gobbled them up without prejudice into an earthly grave behind us.

'Don't look back,' I yelled, waving my friends forward to avoid being swallowed whole.

The tremors soon subsided. I realised most of the prisoners had survived. Gazing back at the giant crater, I sighed.

'Think we are safe now,' Parker said, relieved that the whole ordeal was over.

Chapter Twenty-Five

In the distance coming from the fallen facility was the sound of an army of beating wings and resounding clicks of the night beasts forced from their home.

The beasts blew out into the sky like hundreds of angry cave bats in search of revenge. Chasing down any escapees.

The dark mist that normally masked their approach was no longer, but instead the silhouette shadows of these mighty monsters darkened the skies above.

'I guess run again?' Spencer said, already legging it off towards the marshlands with our crowd of unarmed civilians giving chase in desperate attempts to outrun the terrors of the sky.

They were on us in a flash, swooping down and plucking random people from the ground. We twisted and turned as broken bodies fell out of the sky thudding around us.

It was a massacre! We had no chance unless we got to safety as we had limited weapons and there was no place to hide. The night terrors continued dive bombing, crushing people into the ground and feasting on the victims one by one.

Looking around at my friends, I could see Jessie and Parker. The nimble pair ran together beside me, narrowly dodging ferocious flybys and outstretched claws swinging by their heads. Benji, too tired to run anymore, had hidden in the undergrowth, Lu-Ni was grappling with a beast pinned on the ground avoiding its vicious teeth trying to tear him limb from limb.

Frankie ducked one beast, then grabbed its leg and brandishing her axe, chopped it clean off. She then dropped back down to the floor, doing a commando roll like a pro and continued running for her life.

I was caught by a stealthy stray talon which dragged me up in the air ready to be Gargoyle grub, as Patch tried his best to pull me back only to be taken along for the death ride too. Climbing higher, I looked down helplessly on the battlefield. It was a war we were never likely to win.

My tears started welling up, so many fallen victims and I could tell my friends had run out of luck, penned in and surrounded by this evil flock herding them into a frenzied kill zone.

'Brrrrrrrrrrrrrrrrrrrrrrrrr'

'Brrrrrrrrrrrrrr'

'Brrrrrrrrrrrrrrrrrrrrrrrrrr'

A horn was sounding.

Looking towards the horizon towards the noise, I could see Spencer standing still, way ahead of the pack, gawping at what lay before him.

Tribal armies in formation by the thousand stood before him. They were armed to the teeth with their war banners flapping in the wind.

The cloaking field device around the mountain failed, revealing its true nature. At the front were Queen Ha-Pe's Shibok, leading the charge.

A barrage of precision strikes first came in the form of arrows and spears showering down on the enemy as foot soldiers charged from their lines to save fleeing survivors. Men on buffalo-back charged in from the sides, flanking the massive beasts and forcing them to take to the skies. Above, winged riders on giant crimson condors swooped into the aerial battle, their swift and nimble movements far outmatching their cumbersome foes.

'The cavalry has arrived,' I screamed as my captor was hit in the wing by a harpoon bolt and the tribe below pulled at the rope reeling it in.

In the struggle, I was released from its iron grip and I tumbled towards the floor at breakneck speed. Patch still held on faithfully until the end.

Impact was fast approaching. Out of nowhere Lu-Ni jumped to our aid, catching us mid-air.

'Can't let you die on your first adventure,' he said, grinning at me, before running off to join the fight. I rejoined the rest of my crew, and we watched in delight as the Goodies for once were beating the Baddies in this assault. Colossal catapults could be seen firing webs through the air taking them out like butterflies caught in nets.

'Look over there,' I announced, pointing to Lu-Ni's clan.

The war was raging above us as beast after beast was felled to the floor. It was a perfect military operation destroying these vile creatures from their lands once and for all.

'Now can I say it?' Parker said, nodding at his sis. She nodded back, 'I think we are safe now.'

'Benji you can come out now,' I laughed, spotting his bum sticking out from behind the bushes.

'You'd be rubbish at hide and seek, Benji,' Frankie joined in.

'Did we win?' he asked as he backed out of his burrow still chewing. Even in the face of danger, he never lost his appetite.

Chapter Twenty-Six

The air was hot and sticky. Dust slowly started to settle around us as the storm had passed.

'Anyone seen Patch?' I asked as the little scamp had disappeared.

Parker was also scanning the horizon searching for another member from our new alliance, 'Where is the Lu-Ni-Tic? He's gone too.'

A low rumble incoming on the horizon could be felt beneath our feet. Out of nowhere a big woolly beast came charging towards us. Frankie bravely stepped forward to protect me. She was ready to engage and selflessly pushed me to safety. As she raised her remaining axe ready to tackle the foul wild animal, it slammed on the brakes. The ground shook and crumpled as the beast stopped just inches from Frankie. She slowly lowered her guard as she sensed it meant us no harm.

Frankie could feel its smelly warm breath panting away over her and before she had time to react, it went for the sneak attack. A big sloppy lick, leaving a trail of sticky saliva all over her face.

'Think he likes you,' came the friendly voice of Lu-Ni. His head appeared above Bob's huge thick skull.

'Jeeez,' she moaned as she tried to wipe the saliva off and before she could finish cleaning, little Patch, also riding buffalo-back, ran down Bob's nose to give her another lick for good measure. 'Double jeez,' she moaned again.

'Think Patch is showing how much he likes you too,' I said with a laugh.

'Well, you are lucky! Saliva is supposed to be good for the skin,' added Spencer.

'And looks like you got a lot of it, so your skin will be radiant,' Jessie said, chuckling.

Lu-Ni jumped down to make space for us all, 'All aboard,' he announced, helping everyone up onto the woolly back. 'There is room for everyone.' He ran off to greet his comrades in arms. I watched after him and then I saw Dad again. I kept my eyes on him.

'Dad,' I whispered, as I slid off Bob. I slowly walked towards him. My heart was beating so fast I could hardly breathe. 'Dad... Dad!' I yelled.

'Boo! My boy! Boo!' he cried back to me. We both bolted towards each other. Then we stopped in our tracks.

'It was you. You saved us all. My own son... How?... Why?'

My head was throbbing. Before I could answer he took me in his arms and pulled me into a bear hug. I couldn't breathe again. I couldn't speak. He smelled so good. He was me and I was him. He was everything I missed. My Dad was alive, and a happiness I had never experienced before fell on me.

When he let go of me, he held me at arm's length and then pulled me in for a second hug. This time all the worries and burdens on my shoulders slid right off. It felt so good.

'Mum... is Mum... you know... dead?' I asked choking out the word dead.

'No,' he said, and a sigh fell out of my mouth.

'Where is she?' I asked, frantically searching all around as if she would suddenly appear out of the crowd. Dad leaned over and put his hand on my shoulder.

'I've lost her son. She was taken... but I don't want you to worry as I will find her. I will never stop until I find her.'

'I'll help,' I cried out.

'No, you can't – you are on your own mission. You must complete it. I know you won't want to hear this, but you must leave me here. You simply must. I can't go back with you. Not without your mother.'

Reality hit me hard. Yes, I had found my dad, but he was not coming back with me. He was going to stay and find Mum and there was no way I could imagine him doing anything else. Yes, I wanted to scream and shout and stamp my feet and make him come back with me, but I had to be brave. Mum needed Dad and I had to hold my head up high.

I heard a cough behind me. I spun round. It was Frankie. She had heard the whole conversation. She stepped forward and took my arm. She squeezed it hard.

'I'm here,' Frankie simply said and my heart warmed up. I turned back to my dad and smiled. Something changed in me. I was wiser. I was all grown up.

'Dad, I understand. Go... go and find Mum. Bring her back to me. I promise I will be okay.'

'Are you still with Grandma?'

I swallowed hard. 'No, Dad I am with a foster family.'

His face fell but I quickly said, 'It's okay, they are lovely. I have a little brother called George... and he is sweet and Joyce and my foster dad are great.' I felt guilty saying foster dad, but my real dad smiled as if he understood the guilt.

'It's okay, son. I understand.'

'I see Grandma all the time. She's great!' I added. Dad placed his hand on my cheek.

'Once I find your mum I will be right back. We can be a family again. I'm so proud of you. You look... older. So grown up.'

I was so glad he was proud of me.

Frankie interrupted us, 'He's a great son... and a great friend. He has saved us all. We are all proud of him.'

I smiled as she tucked her hand into my arm.

It was hard leaving dad, but it had to be done. I walked back to Bob and threw my leg up onto his back. I yanked up Frankie who looked concerned for me. I gave her a reassuring smile and a nod.

'My dad must stay for mum. It's the only way.'

She swallowed hard and then nodded back at me.

The six of us straddling the slow plodding giant Bob headed back towards the Shibok's village. We took the scenic route avoiding the dangers lurking in those watery depths from before. I couldn't help but look back hoping to catch another glance of Dad, but he had disappeared.

Suddenly, horns and whistles blared all around us, electric and never-ending. War drums beat to the sound of victory, changed my mood. I began to feel happy again. The tribes did a victory march whilst escorting us back into the jungle.

They proudly dragged their prized kills, caught in the giant nets, behind them. Overhead, bird riders performed aerial displays in perfect formation, celebrating their triumph over evil.

We had won the battle, but the victory felt hollow without Dad to share it with. I wanted him to find Mum and to tell her all that we had done. Then they would both be proud of what I had accomplished, even if they couldn't be here to see it.

'Can't this thing go any faster?' Parker said, impatient to get home.

I looked at Patch for a moment and smiled. I gave him a wink. Patch knew what to do, and moments later he chomped down on one of Bob's bushy tails, igniting the sleeping speed demon into gear. We raced off, leaving everyone in our dust. Holding on for dear life and clinging to each other tightly, we soon pulled into the clearing again for Bob to take his well-earned rest. We all disembarked our living land cruiser and were greeted by hundreds of the happiest faces you would ever imagine. Queen Ha-Pe, despite being old and frail bounced towards us clapping like a satisfied seal.

'Magic dog and magic boy,' she repeated over and over whilst families gathered around to celebrate the return of their adventurous heroes.

We were all flung in the air and paraded around the village.

'I think they are happy,' Parker said, giving a good old grin in appreciation.

'You think,' Jessie replied as we were tossed and thrown jubilantly through the air like ragdolls.

Lu-Ni returned with his tribe, as missing loved ones were reunited with their families once again.

'You know what this means? A feast and a celebration,' he announced as he hugged his mother shedding a tear of delight.

The mystery plaguing these peaceful people was solved for now. The tribes could rejoice and get back to their old lives again.

It was a joyous occasion, and I was proud we were able to bring happiness once again to these kindhearted people. Now it was time to eat. Time to enjoy the festivities and finally go home.

Seated at the head of the great table stump as honoured guests, we were treated not only to a feast for our bellies, but also a feast for the eyes. A circus of celebration was lavished upon us with acrobatics, fire juggling, song and storytelling all depicting our brave adventures. It was a spectacle to behold and something we would cherish forever.

As a special cuisine to mark the occasion, the heads of our vanquished foe were presented in the centre of the table before us. Their once-evil, menacing grins were now the meaty main course, staring blankly back at us from the table. Everyone in Shibok went silent waiting for us to make the first move to eat.

'I think I've turned vegetarian,' whispered Jessie, looking bemused at the heap of heads laid before us.

'Think I'll join you sis,' Parker muttered, 'I think this one blinked at me.'

I told them, 'Don't worry, I'm sure they aren't expecting us to eat this. I believe it is for trophy decoration.' Lu-Ni then shouted out some words to his people to make sure enough more palatable human friendly meals were delivered to our seats.

Benji wasted no time brandishing his oversized knife and fork carving through the meat into neat slices and passing it round, 'I knew these would finally come in handy,' he happily said.

The Shibok all looked at us in amazement as they'd never seen something so civilised. We carefully dished ourselves adequate portions and took the time to savour each tasty mouthful.

Everything was calm, neat, and dignified, just as a dinner table should be. This encouraged a huge roar of laughter from our hosts as the wild pack of hyenas jumped in. They dismantled and devoured anything edible in their eyeline. Food was flying everywhere. Munching, chomping and snorting came from every direction.

'Like happy pigs at a trough,' Spencer said, smiling as he watched the onslaught of carnage on display.

This was the first time away from any real danger and we were all happy that our bellies were full. Deep down, my heart ached for my dad, but I pushed these nagging thoughts to the side. Instead, I decided to praise my partner's part in our thrilling adventure.

'I'd like to say I'm so glad you guys plucked up the courage to come along for this ride. One hell of a rollercoaster ride it's been. Honestly without you, I hate to think what may have happened. I couldn't wish to share my adventures with a better bunch of buddies.'

'Aww, you're going soft and mushy on us, are you, Boo?' Frankie said with a sweet smile. She just knew how hard it was for me to leave my dad. I took a deep breath and she continued her speech, 'I'd also like to add I thought you were all a little dim-witted and complete scaredy cats before, and after this, you've all gone and proved me right.' There was an awkward pause before she winked. 'Only joking, I'm proud to call you my mates, even you Benji.' Frankie patted him on the back making us all smile.

Benji leaned over to give her a high five which she rejected, 'Let's not get too carried away, Sunshine.' She left the poor boy hanging and his face reddened.

Spencer stood up, 'I believe in science, but what I've seen on this adventure has opened up my mind to the possibility there is a lot more beyond our world we are yet to discover.'

Parker questioned him, 'So you believe in magic then - you non-believer. Hmm, I wonder whatever could have made you change your mind?'

'I didn't believe. But cannot deny what I've seen with my own eyes brings me to believe there is more to this universe than what we can comprehend,' Spencer answered him.

Jessie put in her two pennies' worth, 'Oooh, deep, Mr Serious. Can't we just agree we are best mates with an interdimensional superstar hero and a magic dog?'

'With some kick ass friends,' Parker added.

I stood up and said, 'I'll be the first to admit only yesterday we were a bunch of normal kids, but now I believe. We have all been chosen for a higher purpose. Nothing would make me prouder than having you all along as my sidekicks on future adventures. We may have solved this mystery and won the battle, but I have a feeling the war against these dark doers is only beginning. Who will join me?'

Everyone then stood up beside me to make it an official pact.

'Sidekicks, huh? You'll be lucky,' Frankie said, putting her hand straight out in front, 'but count me in, I love a good scrap.'

The twins put their hands forward to join Frankie's, 'All for one and one for all stuff,' Parker said, speaking on behalf of them both.

I joined them, placing my hands in the circle looking over towards Benji who did the same.

'Well, what are we going to call ourselves?' I said, 'Every band of superheroes need a cool name, how about the 'Dark Destroyers' or Special Six? Sorry Patch seven.'

'You can call yourself special,' Frankie said, chuckling out loud.

Spencer then stepped forward, pulling the orb from one of his deep pockets and placing it in the middle of our joined hands

'In the name of science, oh yeah, I forgot I had this thing still, how about 'Protectors of the Light?'' Spencer said, putting his thoughts forward.

'Amazing Spencer, I thought this had been lost forever when everything got destroyed,' I said to him, as we could feel its power surging through us illuminating our faces with its glistening glow.

'I thought it might come in useful and would be a waste leaving it there,' Spencer said calmly.

'The name sounds good too,' I said, looking around at the approving faces and the wagging tail.

'Bravo Spencer, I must say,' Benji said, taking the orb and giving it a little juggle in the air.

'Careful butter fingers,' Frankie said.

I carefully retrieved it from him before he could do any damage and passed it on to Lu-Ni.

'Here, I think this should belong to you. I would like you to protect this with your life and never let it fall into the wrong hands. Hopefully you can use it to keep your people safe. We cannot take it back with us, as our world isn't ready for this knowledge or this kind of power'

'You bring me great honour, Boo,' Lu-Ni said, bowing in gratitude, 'I will miss you and your fellow companions, the light shines bright within you. May it protect you always.'

It was time to say our goodbyes as the day was drawing to an end. I couldn't hide the feeling that I should have stayed and helped dad find mum, but my friends' support helped me to see sense.

'Think it is time to return home,' I announced to the rest, as the partying and celebrations had fizzled somewhat and everyone now was sleepy after gorging themselves senseless into food comas.

Round after round of bowing and hugging and even some crying of happiness followed as we made our emotional exit knowing full well, we'd solved the mystery and saved these people.

Queen Ha-Pe approached me and presented a trinket totem as a gesture of thanks. It was a handmade wooden sculpture of a large dog with six little figures behind it.

'Magic dog,' she laughed to herself, before muttering and passing the trinket to me, 'will look over you.' She patted me on the head before stepping back to give Patch some last-minute attention with a good old belly rub and ear scratch.

Lu-Ni then finally stepped forward to give all of us individual tight hugs. He was teary-eyed the entire time.

'Hopefully your adventures will bring you here again. You will always be welcome at Laridia.'

'Well, do we shake your magic bag and make a wish to be home?' Benji said. We all wondered how we would make the portal appear.

'Sure, Boo knows what he's doing,' Jessie piped up eagerly watching me like a magician about to conjure up a spell.

'Well, it didn't work when he wanted it to the last time,' Parker added with a smirk on his face. I swallowed hard as I knew he might be right. I had absolutely no control over this. Yet it felt like the timing was right.

Frankie was eager to get back. 'How long have we been out here anyway? Not sure I mentioned in all the excitement, but my watch stopped working when I got here.'

Spencer stepped forward, 'Mine stopped too, but by my calculations, two nights and three days, so that means it's most likely Tuesday.'

'Oh my goodness, my parents are going to kill me, I've missed karate training and now missed school, I'm in enough trouble already after the whole dye incident,' she said, running her hand through her hair.

Everyone now started to worry. Surely, we'd be heading back to absolute chaos, with worried parents searching everywhere for us.

I tried to ease the situation, 'Whatever it is I'm sure they'll be happy to see us again. Don't worry we can say we were trapped in the storm.'

'What storm? It never happened,' Parker explained.

Jessie stepped in to say, 'You were the only one Boo who got caught in a storm.'

'The only storm we will get is a tornado of trouble when we get back,' Frankie chipped in.

Spencer looked at everyone and they all looked at him like he would say something inspirational. 'Can we not tell them the truth?'

'Do you think they'd really believe us Spencer? Portals, magic dogs, another world and perhaps a growing evil wanting to destroy the entire universe,' Benji said, 'Sure it would go down a treat.'

'Whatever happens we will stick together. Can we all keep it a secret? Who would believe us anyways? I, for one, am excited for our next challenge. Whatever trouble it gets us into. And I hope you are too,' I proudly said.

We all took a moment staring around at one another. Without words we all knew what the others were thinking. Sheer excitement was plastered across our faces at the prospect of another adventure.

'Well then my fellow Protectors of the Light, if we can overcome the dark, we can easily overcome a few peeved parents, so let's face the storm,' I encouraged the group. It was just as well as a rumble appeared in my pocket. Perfect timing. I peered into the little bag of tricks. Light danced and jiggled around. I watched in wonder as it made its own selection.

'Well, this is new,' I stated as two capsules floated to the surface and into my grasp. Opening up my hand everyone watched in anticipation as the two rolled together, combining into a single ball shape.

'What do red and green do?' Parker asked.

'I think red means home and green means something else I can't quite remember,' I replied.

Looks so pretty,' Jessie said, mesmerised as the swirling colours entwined inside my hand before exploding like a party popper, releasing vivid beauty before the blast of energy

'Here we go again,' Frankie said, steadying herself as the whirlwind cyclone of colour thrashed through the air, lighting up the doorway homeward.

'Well, it's been emotional,' Spencer said straight-faced, stepping into the light as we watched his body disappear into the wormhole.

'Does he ever worry about anything?' Benji said with a laugh before following him through.

The twins held hands and jumped in, 'Weeeeee,' like little children about to take on a water slide.

Frankie was next, but she took a moment to look at me fondly, 'If we don't make it out the other side, I want you to know I've loved every moment. Oh, and thanks for being you.'

She gave me a quick peck on the cheek making me blush. Though she soon quashed the emotion when she followed up with, 'Say a word to any of the others and I'll give you a proper beatdown boyo!' Then she dashed off.

'Well, it's you and me Patch,' I whispered, as I knelt down to give him a warm embrace. He stared lovingly into my eyes, 'I'll try to live up to Jack's legacy, and I promise we'll always make a great team. I can't wait to see what powers you have tucked away for next time. Onwards to more great adventures, my little partner in crime.'

Patch jumped into my arms as we both waved at the shocked Shibok tribe, who were all silent for once. Their mouths were wide open as they watched us slowly slip away.

Chapter Twenty-Seven

'Whoosh!' We were all whisked back to our beloved treehouse. I stepped into the room only to be greeted by the friendly faces of my adventurous team.

We'd all made it back in one piece and our first adventure was at an end.

'What is going on?' I asked, watching Benji who was hopping up and down excited like a hyped-up hare.

We've only gone and done the impossible,' he went on excitedly. 'We are official time travellers. Travellers of time. Wow! And it's only Sunday afternoon,' he added, pointing at his digital watch, which had sprung back to life

'Impossible, but true,' said Jessie and Parker.

'Think we left the impossible behind a long time ago,' Spencer said with a wide grin on his face, 'I think we've broken most known scientific laws already, so add a little time travel too. Why not?'

'Anyone looked outside yet?' Frankie joined in, 'I've seen a few time travel movies where the people return to the world and everything has changed. Either been ravaged by zombie aliens or a great extinction in which we are the only survivors, or-'

'Enough please Frankie. Stop putting ideas in our heads. This isn't a movie. I'm sure everything is fine,' I said, hoping she was indeed wrong.

We all quickly dashed to the edge of the balcony gazing upon our little sleepy town. People were just going about their business.

'Yep, looks as boring as ever.' I announced, a little relieved.

'It's a shame we have to go back to school,' Frankie groaned.

Everyone grumbled at the thought of school in the morning, but were thankful that the world was the same as we had left it. No harm done and most of all no angry parents.

I put the wooden totem memento on the table. It was our first trophy to mark the victory of a grand adventure. Patch stood underneath it, looking up proudly, waiting for acknowledgement.

'Yes, Patch, we couldn't have done it without you,' I said, and his tail wagged with joy.

'I wonder what else you can do?' Parker said, coming closer, 'Fire lasers from your eyeballs, fly like a superdog or spit saliva which burns through metal.' Patch licked his face.

'Confirmed, not burning saliva,' Jessie joked, as Parker's skin wasn't melting away.

'Whatever he is, he isn't your average dog,' Benji added whilst rummaging around in his pockets for a treat, but realised they were empty, 'We've got to go soon. It's dinner time and all this excitement has made me really hungry again.'

Suddenly, I missed Dad. It was like a striking pain in my heart, but then I thought about mum. I knew she needed him. I held my head up high and knew I had to be brave.

'Same time next week then?' I joked, and everyone cracked up in hysterics. Despite the joke, I could see the glint of excitement burning deep in their eyes.

'We are all with you. No one is on their own,' Parker said.

'Until the end,' Frankie added.

Jessie was ready to go too. 'Your secret is safe with us,' she added as she made her way to the rope ladder, dragging her brother behind her.

'It's our special secret. No one else can know,' I called after them, and thankfully they gave me a thumbs-up as they made their way down.

Spencer asked, 'So what time next week? I don't want to be late.' I assured him we would never leave him out.

Departing one by one, my friends disappeared, leaving me alone with Patch on my lap.

'Well old boy, we better get home too.' He let out a short, happy bark. I placed him in the pulley system and climbed down to meet him at the bottom. We marched home with our heads held high and something in my heart told me that new adventures were on the horizon.

Meet the Author

Gary Christopher Boardman, originally from Blackpool, relocated to Southampton in the sunny south of the UK at the age of two, where he has lived ever since.

Gary was a calm child with a vivid imagination and dreamt of setting the world alight one day. With most dreams, reality got in the way, and like everyone else, he had to settle in with the rat race of what is called 'work'.

Becoming a proud father in 2007 gave him the opportunity to feel young again and experience the world again through a child's eyes and rekindle some of that motivation to do something more creative with his life.

As his son grew older, he wanted bedtime story after bedtime story, and to keep up with the boy's desire for adventures, the solution was easy: Gary would weave his own stories on the spot to keep the magic of story time going, nurturing a bond that remains strong even now his son has grown into a teenager.

Whilst he tried his hand at all sorts of make-believe stories and magical adventures, there was one that stood out amongst the others 'Boo & Patch'.

Boo & Patch started out as a simple idea of a boy and his dog travelling through wormholes on different adventures, quickly becoming a nightly request. Gary needed to be on his toes and come up with new story after new story, and with pleasure, he did so.

With much encouragement from his family and setting some personal time aside, he set to the task of bringing these characters to life in his debut book, Boo & Patch, a Tail of Hope, written in 2023 and published in 2026.

As he continues to write, Gary is excited to expand the 'Boo & Patch' series and explore new stories. His journey into the literary world is just beginning, promising more enchanting adventures for readers, young and old.

Follow the Author on Amazon

If you enjoyed this book, tap Follow on Gary Boardman's Amazon author page to get notified when the next book is released. You'll find the Follow button after the last page.

www.ingramcontent.com/pod-product-compliance
Lightning Source LLC
LaVergne TN
LVHW091149080826
845145LV00008B/2308

* 9 7 8 1 9 1 9 5 3 0 1 0 9 *